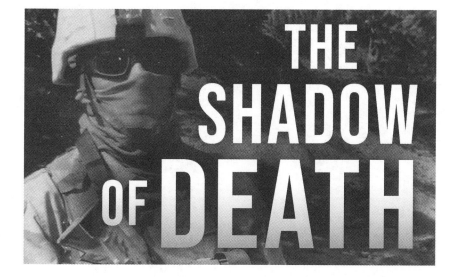

THE
SHADOW
OF DEATH

From My Battles in Fallujah
to the Battle for My Soul

FERNANDO ARROYO

FIDELIS
PUBLISHING

FIDELIS PUBLISHING®

ISBN: 9781737176329
ISBN (eBook): 9781737176336

The Shadow of Death
From My Battles in Fallujah to the Battle for My Soul
© 2022 Fernando Arroyo

Cover Design by Diana Lawrence
Interior Design by LParnell Book Services

For information about special discounts for bulk purchases, please contact BulkBooks.com, call 1-888-959-5153 or email - cs@bulkbooks.com

Fidelis Publishing, LLC Sterling, VA • Nashville, TN fidelispublishing.com

Manufactured in the United States of America

10 9 8 7 6 5 4 3 2 1

This book is dedicated to
Veterans and their families.

Thank you for your service
and thank you for your sacrifice
to this great nation.

.

Contents

Acknowledgments

PRESIDENT RONALD REAGAN said, "Freedom is a fragile thing and it's never more than one generation away from extinction."

It is the less than one percent who answered the call to serve our great nation after September 11, 2001, who keep evil at bay, and secure freedom and the American way of life for so many. Thank you for your service! To everyone I had the privilege of serving with. It was an honor to serve with each one of you. You are truly the greatest human beings I have ever met, and it was an honor to go into battle alongside you.

To my family, thank you for always believing in me and supporting me. To the Ahmanson family, thank you for your continued love and support. You made this possible. To Lela Gilbert, thank you for your patience in working with me to edit this manuscript and supporting me and many other veterans to succeed. To my friend, Marco Hernandez, thank you for encouraging me to write my testimony so veterans may find hope and healing.

To my Lord and Savior, Jesus Christ, thank you for your amazing grace. My story is about my fear and doubt through many trials, and your continued love and faithfulness, even when I wanted to give up.

Chapter One

Torment

IT WAS ABOUT 0800 hours and the smell of burnt human flesh and coagulating blood was overwhelming. I was standing in the rubble that was once an Iraqi police station. Strangely, the smell of human blood brought back to me another odor I remembered from childhood visits to Mexico. My grandpa and uncles were fishermen—casting their nets into the waters of Baja California and catching many fish. The fish had to be descaled and filleted, and I often helped clean them, using a small knife. I was reminded of the way those fish smelled, but I was now staring at what was left of nineteen Iraqi policemen. A suicide bomber drove a bongo truck loaded with 2,000 pounds of explosives into their station. Intermingled and barely hidden within the rubble were the policemen's mangled bodies.

I was fixated on one corpse. I was standing over his body; he was pale blue and partially covered with gray concrete dust from the shattered walls. He had no face, and where he should have had a nose, eyes, ears, and mouth, there was nothing left. A hole providing me with a clear view of what brain matter he had left inside his skull now occupied the space where his face had been. Next to him in the rubble to my right was another Iraqi policeman, also covered in concrete dust and several large pieces of rubble. His face was intact, but his torso contained several baseball-size holes from shrapnel ripping through his body.

~ ~ ~

The events in this book are real, and I have written them to the best of my memory, from my personal experience.

A white ambulance with a red crescent moon on the rear window suddenly appeared to my right. The paramedics backed in close to where more bodies were hidden under the rubble. I watched as two men wearing white collared shirts and black pants rapidly got out and opened the rear double doors of the ambulance. I watched as they removed the Iraqi with the holes in his torso. They picked him up, with one paramedic lifting his legs and the other placing his hands under his armpits. They carried him gently into the back of the ambulance and softly lowered his body. They both quickly jumped out, closed the doors, and ran to the ambulance cab. They turned on the red lights and sirens and drove off.

I watched the ambulance disappear behind tall concrete barrier walls as the paramedics turned left. The sound of the sirens slowly faded away and an eerie silence once again flooded the atmosphere.

"*Allahu akbar!*" The silence was suddenly broken and I immediately realized my life was in danger. I turned toward the sound of the shouting. It came from the third floor of the building across the street from the police station. I saw an Iraqi insurgent wearing a long-sleeved black shirt, a black balaclava, and a tan-colored chest rig with dual magazine pouches. In his arms, he was holding a Dragunov sniper rifle, and his scope was aimed at me. I pivoted to my right to face him and I assumed a good firing stance. I pointed my M-4 rifle at him and I could see the red arrow from my ACOG (advanced combat optical gunsight) center on his head. But I couldn't shoot. My heart was racing and I wanted to squeeze the trigger, but I couldn't do it. My trigger finger had a mind of its own and it would not listen to my brain's commands to fire. I watched as the insurgent aimed at me and squeezed his trigger. I saw his muzzle flash and then I was blinded by a white light engulfing my vision.

"Bravo One One, this is Bravo One Six, over." I could hear my platoon leader's voice coming over my radio, but I could not see or move.

"Bravo One One, this is Bravo One Six, we are taking contact, break . . . there are twenty insurgents armed with AK-47s, RPGs, and

PKM machine guns surrounding our position. You need to get up and fight, over!"

I could hear machine guns and rockets firing all around me but I couldn't see anything but white. *Get up!* I kept telling myself. *You have to fight!* I was screaming in my mind but the words wouldn't come out of my mouth. *Ranger up, and get up!* I raged within as I grew desperate, wanting to fight alongside my brothers. "Get up!" I shouted one last time, but this time the words came out of my mouth and my vision returned.

I opened my eyes and I could see the sights of my 1911 pistol glowing in the dark as I scanned for the sniper who shot me. I wanted to kill him for what he did to me, but I couldn't find him. All I could see was a kitchen. I was in the corner of a room with white walls sitting up on a bed and I was covered in sweat. The room was dark but I could see double closet doors and a tan sofa three feet in front of them. I kept scanning the room for threats but only saw a computer desk in the opposite corner of the room and a television in front of the sofa, next to the bed I was lying on.

It was just another nightmare.

I caught my breath as I felt my heart rate return to normal. I had a headache and was craving a cold drink. I placed my pistol under my pillow where I usually kept it and removed my sweaty blankets. I slid off my bed and put my feet on the carpet. As I stood, I heard bottles clanking and felt one of them land on my right foot. My studio apartment smelled like beer, and the floor was covered in beer bottles after a long night of drinking; I'd gone through about twenty-six of them. I walked toward the kitchen, careful where I stepped, and opened the refrigerator. I grabbed another beer and opened it. I took a long swig from the 16 oz. bottle as the refrigerator air cooled my sweat-covered body.

I stood at the doorway connecting my kitchen to the studio living space and looked around. I hated my life. I felt miserable every day. Why? Because I believed I should have died in Iraq and the best days of my life were behind me.

"God, why did You keep me alive?" I whispered. "I trusted You, Lord, and You failed me. You should have let me die in Iraq."

I walked back to my bed and grabbed the pistol from under the pillow. I pulled the slide back to see if there was a round in the chamber, and there was. With the pistol in one hand and a beer in another, I sat on the sofa. Tears began to roll down my cheeks as I reflected on the possibility of killing myself. I downed the beer and then let the bottle fall on the carpet. The pistol grip felt comfortable in my right hand. It was a model 1911, .45 ACP loaded with hollow points.

The pistol blurred through my tears as I held it in front of me and turned it toward my face. I held it with both hands. The barrel was as wide as my right eye. The tears kept flowing across my cheeks and down my chin. I gently inserted the pistol into my mouth with both hands still on the grip.

Click—the sound of the safety lever being deactivated by my right thumb was loud in the quiet apartment. I could smell and taste the pistol lubricant as I deeply inhaled and exhaled. I placed my right thumb on the trigger and let it sit there.

God, if You're there, save me! I said in my mind hoping God would hear my silent plea, but there was no response. I slowly began to apply pressure to the trigger. I wanted the explosion to be a surprise.

Chapter Two

A Higher Calling

I WAS ENCLOSED in a cloud of smoke as the tires of my gray Dodge Shadow screeched on the pavement of the shopping center parking lot. It was September 11, 2001—a beautiful California morning at 7:30 a.m. and I was late for school.

I was a senior at Bell Gardens High School, but whether I would be graduating that year was questionable. Right then, I was doing donuts in a parking lot near my house and people in the coffee shop there were beginning to take notice. I saw four or five adults standing outside, with their white foam coffee cups in hand, looking at me in bewilderment. I thought it was funny they were watching me, so I poked my head out the window and began to scream in excitement, "Woohoo!"

The men and women shook their heads in disapproval, but I didn't care. I thought it was funny, until I noticed my dad parking his pickup truck in full view of me. In mid-spin I peeled out of the parking lot, hoping he hadn't seen me.

"Damn, that was close," I said to myself.

I arrived a few minutes late to my first class and sat down in the back of the room next to my friend Max. "Did I miss anything?" I whispered leaning toward him.

"Nah, you're good, bro. The teacher was late too. Did you hear what happened in New York?" Max continued, looking toward the front of the class.

"No, what happened?"

"I think a bomb exploded in one of the Twin Towers."

The news didn't mean anything to me. I thought about it for a few seconds and then turned my brain to the teacher to figure out what she was talking about. I quickly got tired of listening to her, and my mind drifted to checking out the girls in class. After what seemed like only a few minutes passed, class was over. The bell rang and I made my way to my government class.

I walked into Mr. Renner's classroom to find him and his students, more or less frozen in their chairs, watching a television set Mr. Renner normally used to show educational videos. I looked at the screen and saw one of the Twin Towers emitting billows of smoke. Then the class gasped in shock as we saw a person appear through the smoke jumping to his death from a high tower window. A few students teared up at the sight of such horror.

"Who would do this?" exclaimed somebody in the back of the classroom.

Then, suddenly, an airplane appeared on the screen, heading straight for the second tower. A girl shouted, "Oh my God!" just as the airplane crashed into the other building, causing a fireball. The seriousness of the situation sunk into my mind and was reaffirmed when a newscaster announced, "America is under attack."

On that day, no more regular lessons took place. Every teacher had a classroom television on, and we watched replays of the attack all day long.

On September 29, 2001, I enlisted in the U.S. Army.

A recruiter took me to the Los Angeles Military Entrance Processing Station (MEPS) where I would receive a thorough medical examination and sign a contract to volunteer for the airborne infantry. After hours of filling out paperwork and being thoroughly medically evaluated, I was sent to a small cubicle where I met with a career counselor. He was a black man with a bald head and reading glasses. He asked me to confirm I wanted to go in the Army.

"I want to be in the airborne infantry, and I want to go to Ranger School."

He looked at me like I was crazy. "Nah, man. You don't want to do that. We got an army cook job which offers a bonus of $20,000." He sounded like a salesman.

"No thanks, I want to be airborne infantry," I told him with a smile on my face. I wondered why he was trying to talk me out of what I wanted. The career counselor laughed and turned to the men in the other cubicles and said, "Hey, this guy thinks he's high speed! Hahaha! He says he wants to be airborne infantry!" The three other men in that small office all turned to look at me and they laughed too.

"It ain't nothin' nice, man," the counselor continued. Now he had a serious look on his face. "Once you sign on that dotted line, there's no turning back. As a matter of fact, have you ever even been on an airplane before?" Now the counselor looked intently at me.

"No, sir, I have never been on an airplane before," I said to him, still with a smile on my face.

"What?" he said in a high-pitched tone of disbelief. "You ain't been on an airplane, and you gonna sign this paper to volunteer to jump out of a perfectly good aircraft?"

"Yes, sir."

"You're crazy, man," and with that exchange, seeing he couldn't talk me out of it, I signed on the dotted line: Airborne Infantry, 82nd Airborne Division, Ft. Bragg, North Carolina.

After signing the contract, I was sent outside to a lobby where I waited to take an oath along with other recruits from the various other branches of the armed forces. I sat next to a shaggy-haired kid from San Luis Obispo. He wore well-used running shoes, faded blue jeans, and an old buttoned-up shirt with a light blue and gray pattern. "What's up, man?" he greeted me.

"Hey man, my name's Fernando, what's yours?"

"My name's Elijah." We sat next to each other staring at the copy of the contracts we just signed. "What's your contract for?" Elijah asked me.

"Airborne infantry. What about yours?"

"Airborne Ranger," he replied.

I was confused. "You mean you're airborne infantry and going to Ranger School?" My recruiter and the career counselor didn't tell me I could get an Airborne Ranger contract.

"It's a Ranger Indoctrination Program contract. It's a contract for the 75th Ranger Regiment, so I'm doing infantry training and airborne school, followed by a three-week course called RIP," he explained.

No one told me there was such a contract. I understood I could volunteer for the 75th Ranger Regiment and Ranger School once I finished airborne training. Anyway, it was too late now!

Once a large group of new recruits filled the lobby, we were all called into a meeting room with light burgundy carpet and white walls, but no tables or chairs. Instead, we lined up in several ranks facing an American flag. A Navy lieutenant stood next to the American flag and said, "You have just volunteered to serve our nation in a time of war. No matter what branch you have joined, or what job you have chosen, you have all volunteered to do something that very few Americans will ever experience. Whether you have a good experience or a bad experience during your service, I promise you that you will forever remember your service as one of the greatest and proudest accomplishments of your life."

I felt chills ripple down my spine as I stood in formation looking at the lieutenant standing next to the American flag. I could not believe I was about to join the Army. It was something I wanted to do since I was five years old.

The lieutenant snapped to attention and said, "Raise your right hand and repeat after me!" Everyone in the room raised their right hands.

"I, Fernando Arroyo, do solemnly swear that I will support and defend the Constitution of the United States against all enemies, foreign and domestic; that I will bear true faith and allegiance to the same; and that I will obey the orders of the President of the United States and the orders of the officers appointed over me, according to regulations and the Uniform Code of Military Justice. So help me God."

After taking the oath, we were all dismissed and told to exit the MEPS building where our recruiters were waiting outside.

"Alright, bro," I said to Elijah, "maybe I'll see you again, but if I don't, good luck."

"Yeah, man, take care. Good luck," Elijah said, followed by a firm handshake. We parted ways and I met my recruiter outside.

"How did it go?" SSG Reyes asked.

"Why didn't you tell me about the Ranger Indoctrination Program contract?" I asked him, feeling like he'd shortchanged me on what I wanted.

"There is only a certain amount of those contracts, and I was told there were no more," he said with a serious look on his face. "Anyway, you can just volunteer for all that cool stuff once you're in. You can even volunteer for Special Forces."

It was a quiet ride back to my house where the recruiter dropped me off. "I'm going to check up on you every so often," he said, "including at your school. Look, you'd better do your work so that you can graduate on time, or else your contract will be canceled."

On June 20, 2002, I graduated from Bell Gardens High School by the skin of my teeth. I managed to avoid being arrested, dying in a car accident, or getting suspended from school, all because I really wanted to serve. SSG Reyes was present at my graduation and, following the ceremony, he shook my hand and said, "I'll see you on August 21, at 0300," then he walked away.

On the night of August 20, 2002, I couldn't sleep. I lay next to my brother, Robert, who was now nineteen years old and listened to him snore all night long as I watched the time go by on the digital clock. At 0300 hours, I was ready to go.

My brother woke up, sat up, and gave me a hug goodbye. "I love you," he said in a low voice. We're not an openly emotional family, except for my mom who has always told me how much she loved me. Once we hugged, my brother laid back down and started snoring again. My mom and dad walked me to the alley behind our small one-bedroom home, where SSG Reyes was waiting to take me to MEPS. Once at the alley, I hugged my mother goodbye as she tried hard not to cry.

"I love you, *mijo*," she said with her voice trembling. "I love you too, ma," I hugged my father and he said, "I love you, son," in a low voice, trying not to show emotion. I got into SSG Reyes's government-issued white Dodge Stratus and off we went.

Once I arrived at MEPS, I saw Elijah. "What's up, bro?" I was happy to see a familiar face.

"You ready to do this?" I asked with a smile.

"I'm ready," Elijah replied. "How 'bout you? You ready?"

"Yeah, I'm ready." A small group of us who were headed for Ft. Benning, Georgia, were taken to Los Angeles International Airport. That's when I started to get nervous. Elijah could see it.

"Are you alright?" he asked as we boarded the airplane.

"I've never been on an airplane before," I said.

"Dude, you're gonna be alright. Don't even sweat it, man."

I sat in the aisle seat next to an older man. He looked about fifty years old, with white hair, and was well-dressed in khaki dress pants and a light blue dress shirt with a blue blazer.

Once the airplane started taking off, I was visibly anxious, even though I tried to stay cool. The airplane began to shake before takeoff and I quickly turned and asked the man next to me, in a startled voice, "Is that normal?"

"Is this your first time flying?" he asked surprised.

"Yes, sir, it is."

"Yeah, this is normal. Just sit back and relax. The airplane engines are gathering thrust for takeoff."

I sat back on my seat and felt my body being pushed back as the airplane took off, and I watched Los Angeles disappear from the airplane window. Once we were in the air and cruising, I looked out the window again and realized why everyone tried to talk me out of being airborne. I was scared and I felt a sense of regret. *I should have listened to my recruiter,* I thought to myself. I volunteered to do something most human beings wouldn't dare do, and now I could see why. As I sat back, I asked God to get me out of this horrible situation. *Why did I sign up for this?*

"What's on your mind?" the man next to me interrupted my thoughts.

"I joined the Army," I replied.

"Wow, that sounds exciting!"

"Yeah, it sounded exciting to me too, until I signed a contract to jump out of a perfectly good aircraft, into battle, even though I've never been on an airplane before!"

"What made you want to join?" asked the older man.

I explained how when I was five years old I watched Operation Desert Storm on television. "I wanted to be one of the soldiers fighting on the ground," I told him.

Then the man asked me an unexpected question. "Do you believe in Jesus Christ?"

"Yes, sir, I do."

"Well, you know," he began, "the Bible is filled with stories of men who faced situations where the odds were against them. Moses, obeying the Lord, opposed Pharaoh, and God used Moses and freed the Israelites. David faced a bigger and more experienced fighter, Goliath, and defeated him. The apostles were fishermen, a tax collector, and a zealot, yet God used them to preach the gospel, and they changed the world."

The man paused as he looked up to the ceiling of the airplane to gather his thoughts, and then he went on, "Did you pray to God and ask Him for His guidance over this decision?"

"Yeah, I did. It started when I was just five years old, and I've been asking about this decision ever since."

"Did God lead you to join the Army?" the man asked, now looking closely at me.

"Yes, He did."

"Then He will get you through this. This will be one of the greatest tests of your faith, but don't lose hope. God is with you."

I immediately felt a sense of peace fall over me. For the remainder of the flight, we got to know each other. He was a lawyer and a man of God. That is all I remember about him.

Chapter Three

Hell's Kitchen

I THOUGHT MY heart was going to jump out of my chest when I awoke to the sound of a fire alarm and flashing white lights. Before I could understand what was happening, I was off the top bunk of my new bed at Alpha Company, 1st Battalion, 50th Infantry Regiment. I heard a voice over the fire alarm shouting, "You're all going to die!"

I landed face down on the highly waxed white tile floor of the barracks, but I didn't feel any pain. Adrenaline was racing through my veins and all I wanted to do was to put on my new running shoes and exit the barracks. As I quickly dressed, I heard a loud crash on the bunk to my left. It was an aluminum trash can flung through the air with dangerous intentions. *I think that was meant to hit me*, I thought to myself before joining the rest of the group, racing out the back door and down the stairs toward the back of the building.

This wasn't combat; it was the first day of infantry training.

Four groups gathered in the field behind the barracks, each with their own designated area. The field was dimly lit by orange-colored lights and was made up of well-trimmed patches of green and yellow grass with large open areas of sand. It was about 0300 hours. The sun was still resting, but my group was about to be put to work.

"Hey, DICKs! Start pushing!" a shadowy figure exclaimed as he was walking with purpose in our direction. I wasn't sure if he was talking to our group, and neither was anyone else, until the figure emerged from the darkness and into the dim orange light. He was six feet tall, muscular, and had beady eyes. He was wearing a brown campaign hat with the U.S. Army emblem centered above the brim and encircled by a thin sky-blue ring. He wore woodland camouflage fatigues and highly shined black jungle boots. Behind him were two more similar figures wearing the same thing.

"I said push, *DICKs!*" he exclaimed in an angrier tone, probably because he didn't want to tell us anything twice. I dropped to the ground with the rest of my group and started doing push-ups. By that time, all four groups were doing the same. Each group was a platoon, and each platoon had their own three drill sergeants.

"My name is Senior Drill Sergeant (SDS) Menifee, and I own your asses! You are now property of the United States government, Department of the Army, Alpha Company, 1st Battalion, 50th Infantry Regiment, 3rd Platoon, Terminators! I want to personally welcome you to Sand Hill, Hell's Kitchen, where killers are made!"

The sun wasn't even up, it was already eighty degrees and the humidity was terrible. I was soaking in my sweat and my arms were already aching from muscle fatigue. The worst part about it was I had only been doing push-ups for about three minutes, and I didn't know how long I would have to do these exercises, or when the day was going to end.

After making his initial introduction, SDS Menifee introduced us to the two drill sergeants who would work under him to make us into infantry soldiers. During his initial introduction both drill sergeants walked around our group, yelling at us to continue pushing through muscle failure.

"Helping me to turn you into warriors is Drill Sergeant Robertson and Drill Sergeant Burdine!" the SDS continued. "Drill Sergeant Robertson and Drill Sergeant Burdine will assist me in destroying each one of you, mentally, physically, and spiritually! Once you are broken, we will build you up into dedicated infantry combat killers! [DICK]"

My arms were quivering, and my chest muscles were burning. I couldn't do anymore push-ups and this caught the attention of DS Robertson. I watched DS Robertson run right to me, jumping over other recruits. I was terrified!

"I guess you thought you could just do whatever you want, huh?" Robertson was bent over at the waist; his campaign cover was inches away from my face and he was pointing at me using his right hand with his fingers fully extended like a knife.

"No, Drill Sergeant!" I replied while trying to push my body off the ground. Now DS Burdine was also bent down at the waist, pointing at me with his own knife hand and yelling in my face. "Hey, DICK! Get your crotch off the f----n floor!"

I don't know how, but I found the energy to lift myself off the ground and continue pushing.

For the next three hours, from 0300 to 0600, I was pressed past my physical and psychological limits. My platoon was put through hell. We were ordered to roll in the sand, then jump to our feet and run in place as hard and as fast as possible. Then we were told to drop to the ground, on our backs, and place our hands beneath our lower backs while alternating our fully extended legs, up and down, to execute what is called a flutter kick. The yelling never stopped, and the drill sergeants never let up on their intensity. Even they were sweating from all the screaming and swarming around recruits who stopped to rest.

After our three-hour workout, we were placed in a marching formation of four ranks and in roster number order. I was no longer Fernando Arroyo; I was roster number three-zero-two (302). Each soldier was paired with another recruit, known as a battle buddy, and the two recruits shared bunk beds and did everything together. If your battle buddy had to use the latrine, then you had to use the latrine. If your battle buddy was punished for being wrong, you were punished for allowing your buddy to be wrong. From the beginning, we were being taught the importance of working together as a team and we were being separated from the civilian mindset of selfishness. My battle buddy turned out to be Elijah, the guy I'd met at the Los Angeles MEPS almost a year earlier. Now he was roster number three-zero-one (301). Together we would have to endure infantry training.

That first day was miserable and our platoon was inside the barracks standing at the position of attention next to our bunks. We were all covered in dirt and sweat, but the drill sergeants did not allow us to shower. In fact, we wouldn't shower for the next week, because one recruit made the mistake of asking SDS Menifee if we would be allowed to do so.

"You wanna be a grunt?!" shouted SDS Menifee, "Then you gotta' smell like a grunt!"

I was standing at attention, along with the rest of the third platoon, wearing my dirty physical fitness uniform and barefoot. My toes were touching a black line running across the barracks in a rectangular shape across the floor, two tile spaces in front of every bunk. This was called "toeing the line" and we learned whenever we were inside the barracks, on the command of "Toe the line," we had to stop everything and stand at the position of attention in front of the bunk with our toes—with or without footwear—touching the black line. We were not allowed to walk in the space beyond the black line of the barracks, which was known as the "kill zone."

It was 2100 hours, and we were preparing for our authorized time of rest called lights out. Now, securely lying in our bunks, and at the position of attention, the men of the third platoon were ready for some hard-earned sleep. It was 2230 and wake up (first call) was 0430, but SDS Menifee had one more requirement before the platoon could sleep. We first have to sing the national anthem.

"On the command of 'sound off' you will—in a loud and thunderous voice—sound off with our national anthem."

He paused for a few seconds. "Sound off!"

The 3rd Platoon Terminators were no choir boys for certain, but in our best Broadway performance voices we sounded off with our nation's anthem.

"That was freakin' horrible!" bellowed DS Burdine.

"Good night, ladies!" exclaimed SDS Menifee followed by the platoon responding in unison.

"Good night, Drill Sergeant!"

The lights were turned off and silence filled the dark barracks room. I was lying on top of my bunk at the position of attention. I desperately wanted to sleep, but I couldn't. My body was aching and I was filled with fear. I realized it was day zero and not day one of training, which meant this long day of pain didn't even count toward the completion of the fourteen weeks left of training. As I lay there on my bunk, looking up at the white foam ceiling tiles, I reflected on my life.

Growing up, my parents couldn't afford to buy my brother and me the better things in life. I wanted Nikes, but I got generic brand shoes. I wanted Levi's jeans, but my dad could only afford cheaper ones. I wanted a bed, but instead we had to sleep on the living room floor. Now, I was in the Army and was issued new Nike running shoes, brand-new boots, brand-new uniforms, I was given three healthy meals, and I had a bed to sleep on. But after day zero, I missed sleeping on that thin blanket, next to my brother, on the living room floor. I would have traded all my new gear for those generic brand shoes and cheap clothes. I wanted my mom's cooking more than chow hall food. I missed my little one-bedroom home and my family. My heart was filled with sorrow and regret.

Lord, I prayed in my mind, *I can't do this. This is too difficult for me. Only You can get me out of this. Help me, Lord.*

As infantry training continued, the challenges became more difficult, culminating in our final, week-long, training field exercise called the Bayonet. The Bayonet ended with a twenty-five-mile road march including obstacle courses and simulated combat missions. The week-long FTX (field training exercise) passed, and the final twenty-five-mile push was beginning. We hadn't had a good night's sleep for five days and we had twenty-four more hours to go. With our fifty-pound rucksacks, weapons, and ammunition, we began the trek to Honor Hill, and it wasn't going to be easy.

At 0000 hours the Bayonet started with combat missions—saving the crew of a downed helicopter, an ammo resupply mission, and an obstacle course. By the time we made it to the obstacle course, we had already walked twenty miles in full combat gear, weighing sixty pounds. Finishing the course meant the beginning of the end of our fourteen week-long journey. We started as scared and timid strangers and were now dedicated infantry combat killers who would slaughter any enemy. We began to cheer as we moved out for the final three-mile stretch.

As we approached Honor Hill, the recruits from other companies lined both sides of the road and cheered us on as we strode up the hill. We were filthy, dead-tired, and all smiles. It was the moment of truth—the moment signifying our official entrance into the infantry. It was nighttime and flaming torches marked the path surrounded by trees and thick brush. Like a secret cult meeting, Honor Hill was reserved only for those who did not quit and endured to the end. Once we arrived, we made a company formation and began to congratulate one another. Then we pulled out our steel canteen cups to receive a cold serving of Powerade. Once every recruit had Powerade, DS Robertson made a toast.

"Only a select few will ever know what it costs to be a member of the most elite fighting force on the planet, and today you are a part of that select few. From this day on, wherever you go, whenever you see another infantryman, he is your brother. You are now part of a brotherhood that has been brought together by patriots who paid the price for freedom with their blood. This we'll defend! To the infantry!"

Once that was said every recruit shouted back in unison, "To the infantry!" and we drank every drop of that ice-cold Powerade.

Next, we were awarded our cross-rifle badge, the symbol of the infantry. The drill sergeants went around to each of their recruits, pinned the rifles on, and punched the pin into each recruit's chest. It was a tradition known as blood rifles. I was no longer a number. I was no longer a recruit. On that morning, around 0100 hours, on Honor Hill, I became Private Arroyo, 11 Bravo.

How did I make it this far? I thought to myself. *How did I find the strength to continue walking all those miles? How did I push myself to these extreme physical limits? What were the chances of me meeting Elijah one year before leaving for infantry training and then ending up being battle buddies in the same platoon?*

My mind quickly shifted from Elijah. Training wasn't over yet, and I had a rendezvous with destiny. I was going to learn how to parachute out of an aircraft into battle.

Chapter Four

Airborne!

IT WAS THE beginning of January and the temperature at Ft. Benning was twenty degrees and falling. The grass was covered by a thin white sheet of ice and the sky was clear. It was 0500 hours and our class lined up in formation in front of the barracks. The instructors were eager to start us out with a five-mile cold-weather run, kicking off the day's events. The instructors, after ensuring the accountability of every student, began to shout the proper marching commands to get three hundred students moving onto the icy road to begin their next journey.

"Double time!" shouted one of the instructors as the entire class shouted in reply "Double time, hooah!"

"March!" and so it began, a five-mile run on an icy road and hilly terrain. After just one mile, my face was numb from the cold. The cold air hurt my lungs as I inhaled through my nose and exhaled from my mouth. My lungs were burning, my feet were numb, and I couldn't feel my hands, but by then I was used to it. Fortunately, fourteen weeks in Hell's Kitchen prepared me for this kind of discomfort.

Just after we reached the second-mile mark, many students began to fall out of the run and refused to continue training. I guess it wasn't just the cold temperature or the pain from the cold air when it entered the lungs. No, it was probably the realization that jumping out of an aircraft from 1,200 feet above ground level in the pitch-black darkness of the night was too great a challenge for them. They were not defeated physically, but psychologically.

When the run was over, we headed for the chow hall. Managing the flow of students into the chow hall was SSG Kelly, and Kelly's favorite thing to do was to humiliate lower enlisted soldiers by making them feel inept. He would point out their mistakes and share his favorite line which was "It ain't rocket science!" to serve as the icing on the humiliation cake he was dishing out.

Even as a lower enlisted soldier, I was cocky, and I couldn't allow such a man, especially a Marine, to torment us lower enlisted soldiers without putting up a fight. One morning after PT, as my company—Charlie Company—was in line to enter the chow hall, SSG Kelly was acting as the door monitor and made it his duty to ridicule the young soldiers by claiming Army physical fitness training was nowhere near as intense as in Marine Corps training.

"I feel like my body was cheated out of a good workout this morning because Army PT is weak!" So said SSG Kelly to a lower enlisted soldier at the front of the line. After a few more soldiers entered the chow hall, I was up next. SSG Kelly kept bad-mouthing the Army as I stood there in silence by the chow hall door, listening to him as he continued his rant on how the Marines were the best branch of the armed forces.

SSG Kelly then looked over at me, standing by the door waiting for permission to enter the chow hall. "Alright, next three students into the chow hall." The door handle was damaged and required a push while opening it. After a quick struggle with the door, I opened it and looked at SSG Kelly with a big smile and I said, "It ain't rocket science, huh, Staff Sergeant?" as I began to step foot into the chow hall. Then, just as my first foot touched the tiles of the chow hall and I had the chance to feel the warmth from the heater, SSG Kelly quickly followed me into the chow hall.

"What? Get your ass over here!" he exclaimed as a fellow Marine stood next to him laughing at what I just said. I was now face to face with SSG Kelly. "Who the f--- do you think you are?" demanded the SSG. He could not believe someone of a lower rank and from an "inferior branch" of service would dare speak to him in such a way.

"I'm Private Arroyo," I said in a calm voice. The lack of fear in my voice and my almost arrogant posture—my chest sticking out and my back erect in an exaggerated form of the position of parade rest—only infuriated SSG Kelly more.

"Start pushing, smart ass!" he exclaimed. "I hope you like eating last because from now on you're always going to be the last in line."

I pushed away in the freezing cold. I still had a smile on my face, but I knew I started a battle with a tyrant and there was no turning back. Only after the rest of the class entered to eat did SSG Kelly give me permission to enter the chow hall. As I got up and approached the door, SSG Kelly stood in front of me and said, "I'm gonna make your life a living hell."

"Thank you, Staff Sergeant," I replied. "I'm looking forward to it."

SSG Kelly could not believe what he was hearing. He wasn't used to being challenged in this way, but I wasn't one to allow anyone from another branch of the armed forces to ridicule the greatest branch of them all—the U.S. Army.

One day, after training was complete, SSG Kelly summoned me to enter his presence. "Your day's not over, Arroyo. Everyone can go, but since you want to be such a smart ass and have the energy to run your mouth, I'm gonna smoke your ass so you learn to keep your mouth shut." He had a large grin on his face.

"You can't smoke me, Staff Sergeant," I replied in an overconfident tone. For the next hour and a half, SSG Kelly ordered me to execute several exercises meant to cause fatigue and, ultimately, muscle failure.

As sweat dripped down my face and my body was elevated over a puddle of sweat, I heard a voice of reason and authority in a stern voice that conveyed authority over SSG Kelly. "That's enough for today, Staff Sergeant." It was Army Staff Sergeant Eton, a Ranger qualified infantry-man who served in a Long-Range Surveillance Detachment in Germany.

"Save that s--- for tomorrow," SSG Eton told SSG Kelly.

SSG Kelly did not want to argue. "See you tomorrow, smartass," he barked, and with that he walked away.

"Get up, Arroyo." SSG Eton wore a shaved head, Army-issue tactical prescription glasses with black circular frames around the lenses, and a black plastic strap that wrapped around his head. I got up and stood at parade rest in front of him.

SSG Eton also wore the Expert Infantryman's Badge (EIB) so I knew he was a fellow grunt. "Grunt, huh? F--- the Marines. Obey the orders of your superiors, but never quit and never give up."

"Yes, Sergeant."

"Fall out." And with that I walked away.

Every day began at 0500 and ended at 1700 or later, depending on the training. Those days were long and brutal, but it was necessary to make the procedures for exiting an aircraft and landing safely into muscle memory. Every day, for the first two weeks, a few but not many students quit training because of the mounting fear of the danger ahead. But as other students quit, I was looking forward to extracurricular training from SSG Kelly, who remained eager to destroy me.

Every night at airborne school there were several exits and entrances throughout the barracks the students had to guard throughout the night to maintain a safe resting environment for everyone inside. It was not uncommon for students to attempt sneaking in a night of partying along the notorious Victory Drive in Columbus, Georgia. One Saturday night I was not awakened for my guard duty shift. The soldier on the previous guard shift claimed he woke me up, but it was a lie. The guard duty officer in charge (OIC) noticed during his walk through the barracks the back entrance was unmanned. He quickly ran up the stairs and woke me at 0300. I was sound asleep when I felt my entire body shaking in what I thought was an earthquake.

"Wake up!" shouted the OIC. You're late for your shift!" I quickly got up and, in what seemed like a split second, I put on my battle dress uniform (BDUs) and boots and ran to my guard post. "We'll talk about this later," the OIC told me.

I felt a surge of anxiety as he walked away. The realization that I could be removed from airborne school was lingering in my head like a bad smell lingers in the air. But what really bothered me was knowing SSG Kelly was now going to have more reason to torment me. There would soon be a painful consequence. I would have to pay for my mistake, even though it was the previous soldier on guard duty who hadn't wakened me.

It was Monday morning, and we were assembling for formation. I wanted to be one of the first to arrive to avoid being seen by SSG Kelly, who was usually inside the barracks making sure everyone was on time. It seemed like a regular start of the day and a feeling of relief came over me as I (foolishly) thought maybe no one really cared I missed my guard shift that Saturday morning. It seemed like no one knew what happened until I heard SSG Kelly's shout. "Dammit, Arroyo!"

All hell was about to break loose. SSG Kelly, SSG Eton, Corporal Hence, and an instructor were all walking toward me as I was standing in formation wishing I could just disappear.

"Why were you late, Arroyo?" asked Corporal Hence. CPL Hence was a member of the Force Reconnaissance Marines, an elite unit in the Marine Corps whose mission was to conduct long range recon and direct-action missions. Unlike SSG Kelly, CPL Hence was a calm, no-nonsense, guy.

"I was not woken up for my shift, Corporal."

"If you were in a foxhole in the front lines you would have had your buddies' throat slit because you failed to do your guard shift, airborne!" shouted the Black Hat.

"Yes, Sergeant, Airborne!"

"Your ass is gonna pay for this, Arroyo. I'm going to make sure that you suffer for what you did," said SSG Kelly in an angry tone carrying with it a sense of satisfaction that he was going to enjoy inflicting more pain on me.

The second week passed without punishment for my transgression, but SSG Kelly had only been waiting.

"Where's Arroyo?" I heard SSG Kelly shout. "Get your ass over here!"

I was exhausted from the second week's events and was not looking forward to the additional physical torment he was about to inflict on my body.

"You thought I forgot, huh?" asked SSG Kelly with a huge grin on his face.

"No, Staff Sergeant," I replied.

"Front leaning rest position! Move!" And so began a series of physical exercises meant to painfully teach me there is no excuse for failing to perform my duties.

SSG Kelly lit up a cigarette as he watched the sun setting over the horizon. Students were leaving the barracks in their civilian clothes, on their way to have fun over the weekend. He took long, slow drags from his cigarette and then inhaled slowly, savoring the taste of the tobacco before exhaling a cloud of smoke into the air. It was not clear whether he was truly enjoying the sunset, or simply embracing this long-awaited moment in which he could make me miserable. I felt the sweat dripping down my face.

"Flutter kicks," said SSG Kelly in a calm voice. I glanced at SSG Kelly's eyes and he showed no emotion of any kind. For him, at that moment, the pain being inflicted on me was nothing personal, but simply business.

After an hour or so of corrective training, SSG Kelly ordered me to squat and remain in the squat position with my knees bent at a ninety-degree angle and my arms straight out in front of me with my palms facing down. I remained in that position for several minutes as my body began to shake violently as muscle failure was looming. The sun set and SSG Kelly remained quiet as the sound of me grunting in pain was the only noise to be heard in the cold night air.

"Recover," he snapped. I stood up, slowly, at the position of parade rest in front of the staff sergeant. Sweat dripped down my face and the cold air began stealing the heat from my body. I could see steam from my body heat leaving my uniform.

"Relax," said SSG Kelly. I didn't know how I should stand, so I stood at the position of "at ease" with my hands still behind my back.

"Where you from?"

"California, Staff Sergeant," I responded as I was beginning to catch my breath.

"Whereabouts?"

"Bell Gardens, Staff Sergeant."

"Where the hell is that? Some f---- ghetto?"

"It's near East Los Angeles, Staff Sergeant."

"What job did you sign up for?"

"Airborne Infantry, Staff Sergeant.

"So you wanna be a hell raiser, huh?" SSG Kelly now had a grin on his face. It was a casual conversation he wanted to have, but I couldn't help but think there was still more physical torment to follow so I kept my guard up.

"I wanna fight the enemy, Staff Sergeant."

"You're a good soldier, Arroyo. You would have made a great Marine." I was taken aback. "Enjoy your weekend." SSG Kelly then turned casually and walked away. He never messed with me again.

~ ~ ~

It was week three and time to finally jump out of an aircraft. That Monday morning started like every other day. I woke up at 0500 and made my way to the latrine to expel unnecessary bodily fluids, followed by brushing my teeth and shaving. Since there were many airborne students, to expedite the hygienic process, two or even three students shared a sink at any given time. I happened to share mine with SSG Kelly. As we were both scraping the hair off our faces, SSG Kelly decided to talk about the elephant in the room.

"Y'all realize we're gonna jump out of a perfectly good aircraft while in flight today, right?" The atmosphere in the latrine was transformed from students attempting to go about the day as if it were any other day, to having to contemplate the dangers of airborne operations.

Our nervous thoughts were soon replaced by action. There was no amount of training or simulation that could replicate the actual process of parachuting out of a C-130 Hercules at 130 knots over a landing zone at 1,200 feet. And the fact it was a matter of life and death could not have been stressed more by the instructors. After receiving all the necessary equipment, it was time to "rig up." Each student was partnered with another, and we proceeded to secure our airborne buddy with the harness, parachute, and reserve parachute, just as we were trained to do for the last two weeks. After every student was rigged up, the Black Hats began to perform their Jumpmaster Personnel Inspection (JMPI).

Once the aircraft arrived at the airfield, we were ordered to stand and proceed into the aircraft, through the rear door. As I entered, the hot air from the propellers added to my discomfort as I sat on the very uncomfortable nylon seats. Once every student was seated, the rear door was closed, and the aircraft began its ascent into the cold Georgia sky.

When this airplane lands, I'm not going to be in it, I reminded myself.

Once in the air, it seemed like just a few seconds went by as the jumpmasters began to deliver their commands to us in preparation to exit the airplane. "Twenty minutes!" the instructors yelled simultaneously as they stood by the left and right rear doors of the aircraft.

Once everyone was standing with their static lines hooked to the cable in the aircraft, the command of "Standby!" was given.

I was "standing by" behind several other students, waiting for the command to exit. "Green light go!" was the final command given by the jumpmaster, and one after another I watched as each soldier in front of me jumped out the door, sucked out like he was disappearing into a vacuum. When I finally reached the door, there was no hesitation, and I cast myself into the mercy of God and His airspace at 1,200 feet above the ground. As I threw myself out of the rear left door, I felt the shock of the 130-knot winds push against my body as I began to count: "One thousand, two thousand, three thousand, four thousand!"

I felt that jolt as my parachute opened behind me and caught the air. It was the greatest feeling of relief I had ever experienced. I could see other students hovering in the air as we ascended to the earth.

I landed with ease and great relief. I took off my parachute, put it away in my kit bag, and made my way to the student collection area. Then I watched another class exit their C-130 and take the same trip back to earth I just experienced. There was nothing like the feeling of finally landing. It produced a sense of confidence immediately making me want to jump again. The adrenaline rush was like nothing else I ever experienced. I jumped four more times including two at night, executed in full combat gear weighing in at about 120 pounds. Once it was all over, we were driven back to the barracks and allowed time to sleep and prepare for the next day.

On the second to last day of airborne school, we were ordered to clean out the entire barracks. While I was cleaning my barracks room, CPL Hence came by and said, "You still owe me for failing to complete your guard duty shift, Arroyo." CPL Hence was six feet, two inches tall and weighed about 175 pounds. By this point, after enduring such torment from the Black Hats and SSG Kelly, I was always ready for a smoke session.

"Follow me," said CPL Hence. We walked up stairs to the vacant third floor and entered a large barracks room containing four army bunks and several empty wall lockers. Since heat rises, the third floor felt like an oven and we were sweating just from the walk up the stairs.

"These are your options, Arroyo," the corporal said in a professional business tone. "You can either do two extra guard shifts tonight for a total of one and a half hours of guard duty, starting at 0200 to make you lose sleep; or I can smoke you right now for the next hour and call it even. The choice is yours."

I knew the right answer. I was trained by my drill sergeants in Hell's Kitchen. It was only through pain grunts learned what was right and what was wrong.

"Smoke me, Corporal."

"Take your field jacket off and get in the front leaning rest position," said CPL Hence.

From behind the corporal, and standing in the hallway, the voice of Staff Sergeant Eton exclaimed, "Outstanding! That was the right answer. That's how a grunt must respond!"

And so it began. A one-hour-long, Force Recon Marine, smoke session. I performed countless lunges and squat jumps up and down that barracks room. As usual, my uniform was soaked in sweat and my muscles felt that all-too-familiar burning sensation from the tearing of their tissue as they were being pushed past their physical threshold. Once the hour was over, CPL Hence simply handed me my field jacket and said, "Good job."

I was debt free and able to enjoy my last moments at airborne school in peace.

When graduation day came, I was proud. I faced my fear. And against every natural human desire for safety and security, I threw myself out of a perfectly good aircraft, by day and night, in preparation for my future operations as a paratrooper. The graduation ceremony was brief with a short speech given by the regimental commander, followed by the pinning of the U.S. Army Jump Wings on our chests. Immediately after the ceremony, I grabbed my duffel bags and boarded a bus headed for my new home, Fort Bragg, North Carolina, the home of the Airborne and Special Operations Forces. I was about join the 82nd Airborne Division, 1st Battalion 505th Parachute Infantry Regiment. The 82nd Airborne maintained a reputation within the Army as being both an extremely aggressive unit and an elite global rapid deployment force always ready to deploy anywhere in the world, within eighteen hours of notification.

This was where the rubber would meet the road.

Chapter Five

Bravo KI, March or Die!*

IT WAS A familiar scene. Once again, my reflection on the highly waxed white tile floors of the Bravo Company barracks became blurrier with every drop of sweat dripping off my forehead and every push-up I completed. I arrived at Fort Bragg and was assigned to the 1st Battalion 505th Parachute Infantry Regiment, Bravo Company, 1st Platoon. I was ordered to do push-ups, lunges, and sprints up and down the hallway of the barracks for the last hour, and there seemed to be no end in sight. All the men of 1st Platoon stood along the sky-blue painted walls of the hallway and cheered for me as I endured this latest physical torment my new squad leader, Staff Sergeant Ryans, was inflicting on me.

This time it wasn't hazing. It was a test of endurance meant to measure my grit and resolve as a new paratrooper in the ranks. First Platoon had just returned from a seven-month deployment to Afghanistan where they worked alongside Special Forces and the special missions units of the Army and Navy, to kill or capture Taliban and al-Qaeda fighters in the rugged mountains of the Hindu Kush.

After seven long months in combat, each member of the 1st Platoon knew and trusted each other. It was more than a friendship; it was a brotherhood unlike anything a civilian could experience or understand. To become a member of this brotherhood was no easy task, and I would have to sacrifice my neurological instincts of self-preservation,

---

* 1-505 B Co. slogan.

while placing the lives of my new family before my own. And it all began with this test of my grit.

"Get up and stand at attention, Arroyo," said SSG Ryans in a calm voice, with a Kentucky-style Southern accent. Two hours passed and I made it through another grueling test of my endurance. I stood at attention.

"Ascencio!" exclaimed Ryans as he stared me down like a drill sergeant looking for a flaw in a recruit's uniform. Out of a barracks room and into the hallway came a six-foot two-inch-tall paratrooper with a big, muscular frame. His uniform was perfectly pressed with clean crease marks running down both of his sleeves and pant legs. His boots were shined like black mirrors. The young specialist approached SSG Ryans confidently and then stood at parade rest.

"Yes, Sergeant," said Ascencio.

"This is your new Joe so make sure he gets squared away. Help him get his gear from supply and make sure he has his load bearing equipment (LBE) ready for the jump tomorrow."

"Roger, Sergeant," replied Ascencio, and with that SSG Ryans left for a meeting at the first platoon office.

"So let's walk to supply and get you squared away."

"Yes, Specialist," I replied while standing at parade rest.

"You can just call me Ascencio. Where are you from?"

"California."

"Where in California?"

"I'm from Bell Gardens. It's a small city not far from East LA."

"That's cool, man; my wife and I are from Anaheim."

We spent a few hours getting my gear ready for the airfield seizure training exercise the next day. We were going to parachute into an enemy airfield and take the airport by force.

"Be ready tomorrow at 0430. It's going to be a long day so get some rest because we won't sleep again for the next twenty-four hours."

"You got it!"

Chapter Six

OOPS!

"ONE MINUTE!" YELLED the jumpmaster, and every paratrooper echoed the command. There was strain on my shoulders from the more than 130 pounds of equipment I was carrying. Fifty pounds is the average rucksack weight, but with a parachute, reserve parachute, radio batteries, water, and extra ammo belts for the M240B machine gun teams (since we were tasked as the support by fire platoon, SBF), the weight was much greater in this role.

"Thirty seconds!" I could feel the aircraft making final adjustments as the pilot aligned the plane properly onto the approaching drop zone (DZ).

"Stand by!" LTC Drinkwine handed his static line to the jumpmaster and stood ready as he propped himself in front of the exit door with the wind violently whipping his uniform. In the airborne, leaders jump first, from the highest-ranking officer down. The idea is paratroopers lead by example.

"Greenlight GO!" yelled the jumpmaster, signaling the aircraft was now over the LZ. With the command of "Go," LTC Drinkwine disappeared into the night as he hurled himself out of the aircraft.

One after another, each paratrooper before me disappeared into the night sky. Finally, without hesitation but a little ripple of fear, I handed my static line to the jumpmaster and threw myself out of the aircraft. The cold air swept my body into the night sky as I flew just feet away from the skin of the aircraft. "One thousand, two thousand, three thousand, four thousand!" I yelled, praying to God I would feel the tug from my parachute stopping my uncontrolled descent to the earth. I felt the tug and the G-force of the parachute catching the wind and rapidly slowing my descent. Once my parachute opened, a peaceful silence filled the night. I could see the shadows of the open canopies of paratroopers raining from the sky.

I landed on the runway of the airfield and hit the ground hard, like a sack of potatoes. I took off my parachute harness, packed it in my kit bag, and dropped it off at the parachute turn-in point. I then ran to the support-by-fire position, only to find I was the only one there. I felt a sense of accomplishment since I was the new paratrooper and yet managed to reach the support-by-fire (SBF) position before everyone else. A few seconds later the three machine gun teams arrived and took up positions, with each machine gun targeting a building. Once they were set, all hell broke loose.

The machine guns, each having over two thousand rounds of ammunition, began to fire at a cyclic rate of fire for three seconds and then lowered their rate to a rapid-fire pace, firing five-round bursts, one after another, in what they called "making the guns talk." Then the rest of 1st Platoon arrived and every squad assigned their paratroopers specific buildings and specific floors to engage.

Everything seemed to be going great until Ascencio came over to me and laid in the prone position next to me.

"Arroyo! Engage building two, third floor!" he shouted over the loud gun fire.

"Roger that!" I replied as I squeezed on the trigger of my M-4 and released several rounds into the third floor of the building.

"Turn on your PAQ-4!" shouted Ascencio.

Every grunt had PVS-14 night vision goggles that enabled us to see the PAQ-4 infrared aiming light. I reached to turn on my rifle-mounted PAQ-4 infrared aiming light.

It wasn't there.

"Hurry up and turn it on!" shouted Ascencio.

"I can't find it."

Ascencio grabbed my rifle and inspected it.

"Oh no." His tone of voice was not reassuring.

A PAQ-4 is what is referred to in the Army as a "sensitive item" and it is no different than a rifle scope or the rifle itself. If anyone loses any of these sensitive items in training, all training must stop and every paratrooper is required to walk around the entire training area, inspect every vehicle and even the aircraft until the item is found. This missing infrared laser on my rifle could potentially stop the entire 1,200 paratrooper airfield seizure exercise and permanently place me on everyone's hate list. The stakes were high and immediate action had to be taken.

Ascencio made his way to SSG Ryans and informed him of the situation. In the process of informing SSG Ryans, Sergeant First Class Nelson, the platoon sergeant, overheard.

"Whaaaat! You better find that PAQ-4 before I start cracking skulls and kicking all of your asses!"

Ascencio was the best team leader in the platoon and SFC Nelson trusted him and held him with high esteem. "Ascencio, I'm counting on you to make this right. I know you can find it. I'm counting on you. Fix this."

"Yes, Sergeant." Ascencio came back to me and he asked me,

"Where did you land?"

I remembered exactly where I landed because it was on the hard surface of the airfield runway and it hurt. "I landed on the runway just a few hundred meters from here. It's a spot next to a gas station."

"Okay, take me there," replied Ascencio with a professional tone expressing a serious sense of urgency.

First Platoon, 2nd Squad, Bravo Team was tasked with finding the PAQ-4 I lost, so all four of us made our way to the runway as they followed me. As we headed toward the runway, we moved in the darkness, able to see everything in night vision green.

"This is the spot where I landed," I told Ascencio. We began to walk around the area staring at the ground hoping to see the little black rectangular laser pointer through our night vision. I looked up and saw a figure of a tall and muscular man coming our way.

"Who is that?" I asked Ascencio.

"Oh no! It's Command Sergeant Major Lambert."

CSM Lambert was the battalion command sergeant major and not one to be crossed. Standing at six feet, three inches, and weighing in at about 230 pounds of muscle, he looked like a professional bodybuilder. His biceps were bigger than the heads of most paratroopers.

"Hey, airborne! What unit are you with?"

Our entire fire team was compromised and there was only one thing we could do—act like we were lost.

We don't know where we are, Sergeant Major," replied PFC Wilcox.

"We're with B Co., 1st Platoon, Sergeant Major," replied Ascencio.

"You need to be on that hill. That's where the support-by-fire position is."

"Yes, Sergeant Major, and thanks for the help," said Ascencio trying to sound sincere.

We began to move back, but as soon as CSM Lambert went another direction, we turned back around, this time with an even greater sense of urgency. We made our way back to the runway, near the gas station, and continued searching for the missing PAQ-4. Ascencio saw what looked like a black box sitting on the dirt road.

"I got it!"

As I approached Ascencio I had a big smile on my face. I put my hand out to get the PAQ-4 that fell off my weapon and almost caused an entire battalion training exercise to come to a halt.

"Can I have that?"

"No, I've got it. Let's head back," replied Ascencio quietly. My sense of relief began to fade.

By the time we returned to the SBF, the training exercise had ended.

"I found the PAQ-4, Sergeant."

"Let me see it," replied SFC Nelson.

SFC Nelson ordered Ascencio to attach the PAQ-4 back onto my rifle and to secure it with 550 Cord. After that, I was told, "Go see the First Sergeant on the LZ, he has a special job for you," said SFC Nelson with a look of disapproval on his face.

I can't believe I let everybody down, I thought. I was disappointed at myself. *Now I'm on the turd list for sure!*

I reached the 1SG's location and there I saw three other paratroopers taking a knee in a horseshoe formation around the 1SG and the company commander, Captain Cerino.

"First Sergeant, Private Arroyo reporting as ordered."

"You're the damn new guy that almost caused this entire training exercise to stop!" replied the 1SG in an angry voice.

"You're the son of a bitch that almost f----- up the entire training exercise," CPT Cerino stated in a matter-of-fact way.

"Yes, sir."

"You moron! You messed up tonight. So while the rest of the battalion catches a ride home, turns in their weapons, and gets a hot shower, a hot meal, and well-deserved sleep, you will stay out in this God-forsaken drop zone and collect all the parachutes stuck in the trees. You're on chute recovery detail, so get used to it because it might take you the next twelve hours to finish."

As I walked toward the Humvees on the drop zone, another Humvee drove up to our group. Two young Puerto Rican lieutenants were in the front of the Humvee.

"Hey, what is your name?"

"Private Arroyo, sir."

"Okay, Arroyo, get in."

"Yes, sir," I replied and I jumped into the back of the Humvee and we sped off.

The lieutenant at the Humvee's wheel was driving like a maniac. Maybe he was testing the vehicle's off-road capabilities, or maybe he was just a maniac. Either way he began to ask me questions about where I was from and where my parents were from. It turned out both lieutenants were from Puerto Rico and they thought that I might be too. That's why they'd invited me to get into the Humvee with them.

"So where are we going?" I asked, as I bounced from side to side in the rear of the Humvee with all four wheels often leaving the ground.

We're taking you back to the barracks.

"I thought I was on chute recovery detail?"

"Do you want to go home or do you want to stay out in the wood line collecting parachutes?" asked the driver.

"I would rather go home, sir."

"*Entonces no jodas mang!*" and with that, I sat back in the Humvee, that stopped bouncing around because we reached a hardball road. I closed my eyes for a quick nap.

"Hey, Arroyo, wake up."

We were back at the B Co. barracks and I was dropped off. The two lieutenants sped off and I never saw them again. I walked up to the barracks and everyone was in company formation. I found my place with my squad as 1SG Whomack and CPT Cerrino were giving their motivational speeches, telling the men what a great job they all did. Once it was over, everyone in 1st Platoon turned to look at me.

"Why are you not on chute recovery detail?" asked SFC Nelson.

"They said they didn't need me, Sergeant."

"After that s--t you pulled tonight, I should drive your ass out there myself and leave you in the wood line."

"Yes, Sergeant."

There was nothing else I could say to SFC Nelson's comment. At this point, I knew God must have been looking out for me because I dodged a horrible night of climbing trees to set parachute canopies free from the branches they were stuck to.

This is amazing grace! I thought to myself as I entered the barracks, and turned in my rifle and night vision into the arms room. Then I saw Ascencio walking toward me and my heart sank. I braced myself for what he was about to say.

"It was my fault, Arroyo," were the first words out of his mouth.

"No way, Ascencio, I failed to maintain accountability."

"No, the 550 Cord was rotten. It was worn out during the deployment to Afghanistan in the mud and in the cold weather. It needed to be replaced and I failed to inspect it during my pre-combat checks and inspections."

I couldn't believe it. I realized right then I was in the presence of a true leader. Ascencio made no excuses for himself, even when it was easy to pass on the full blame of the incident to me. I was "the new guy," who had no credibility among a group of warriors who trusted each other like brothers.

"Arroyo!" My name echoed down the barracks hallway of the 1st Platoon area. It was the familiar voice of the platoon sergeant, SFC Nelson.

"Moving, Sergeant!"

I ran past the paratroopers who were loitering in the hallway just waiting to be dismissed for the day so they could enjoy a hot shower and rest. It was 0100 hours, and everyone was exhausted.

"Yes, Sergeant."

I was standing at parade rest and waiting to hear what SFC Nelson had to say.

"You f----d up tonight, but you're still okay. I saw that the 550 Cord was old and rotten from underneath the PAQ-4, so you couldn't have seen it unless you took it off your weapon. I'll give you the benefit of the doubt. Oh, and you're fired. Tomorrow you're trying out for a different platoon."

I didn't understand what SFC Nelson was talking about or why a platoon would require "tryouts."

"You're going to report to the third floor of the Charlie Company barracks. Report to SFC Bailey. He is the Scout platoon, platoon sergeant. Good luck." SFC Nelson shook my hand and walked away.

I made my way to Ascencio and asked him, "What is the Scout platoon?"

"Why do you ask?"

"SFC Nelson told me that at 0900 hours tomorrow I'm trying out for the Scout platoon."

"What?!" Ascencio looked astonished. "Dude, the Scout platoon is the reconnaissance platoon for the battalion, and only the best paratroopers are chosen to be a part of it. They're all required to attend

Ranger School and they all get to train as snipers, and some of them have already passed the Special Forces Assessment and Selection course. If you make it into the Scout platoon, you'll be in a better place than this, and that's for sure. Good luck!"

If I made it through the two-week tryouts, I would be a member of a recon team operating in teams as big as six, and often as small as two, whose mission was to move behind enemy lines. It was 0200 and the platoon was dismissed until 0900 the following day. After a hot shower, I was on my bed but I couldn't sleep. I recalled the night's events, and I couldn't make sense of any of it.

Meanwhile, in those sleepless minutes, I wondered if I would make it through the two-week tryouts, or would I return to 1st Platoon with my head bowed in failure. There was nothing I could do now. I'd just have wait to be given the chance prove to myself—and to the men of the Scout platoon—that I had what it takes to join their ranks.

God, give me the strength, because I can't do this without You. Amen.

Chapter Seven

Tryouts

ON THE THIRD floor of the Charlie Company barracks, the skull on the wall was looking back at me as I stood at attention. It was a white skull with a crossed paddle and rifle replacing the usual crossed bones. Above the skull was a black and gold Ranger Tab and below the Ranger Tab was a Ranger scroll that read "82nd ABN–Recon 1-505 PIR." The backdrop was black and surrounded by army green camouflage netting.

I arrived at the Scout platoon headquarters for tryouts at 0900, and I was told by a young NCO (non-commissioned officer) to stand at attention in the center of the Scout platoon hallway, and to wait for further instructions. The hallway was empty and looked identical to that of the B Company's 1st Platoon barracks—brick walls painted sky blue, and white tile floors waxed to a gloss. I could hear several voices in the Scout platoon office down the hall, but I couldn't make out what they were saying. Then the door swung open and the young NCO, who previously ordered me to wait in the hallway, stuck his head out of the doorway.

"Hey, dude, come in."

"Yes, Sergeant," I replied as I double-timed to the office.

The office consisted of a simple layout. Toward the wall to the left of the door were two bulky metal office desks, and sitting behind each one was the platoon sergeant and the platoon lieutenant. In front of the desks and closer to the door was a table with eight chairs, already occupied by seven volunteers. The walls of the office bore camouflage netting. Gray wall lockers for storing equipment lined a couple of them. I stepped into the office and stood by the desk, next to the other seven volunteers, at the position of parade rest.

"Come up here, Private," said the platoon sergeant, SFC Bailey.

He was a muscular black man and his uniform was perfectly pressed. At the desk next to his was the platoon leader, Lieutenant Zawachesky (Lt. "Z"). Lt. Z had blond hair and green eyes with an athletic build. He gave off a slight glow of arrogance as he leaned forward on his chair and rested his arms on his desk.

"How old are you?" asked SFC Bailey.

"Eighteen years old, Sergeant."

"You think you got what it takes to be in the Scouts?" asked Lt. Z with an arrogant smirk on his face.

I could see the doubt in Lt. Z's eyes. It seemed the Lieutenant wasn't so sure an eighteen-year-old kid, who just finished infantry and airborne training, was the kind of paratrooper they were looking for.

"I have what it takes to be in the Scout platoon, sir."

I answered Lt. Z's question and I added an arrogant smirk of my own. Not everyone volunteers to parachute out of an airplane into a combat zone. It takes a certain type of person to do this type of work. After surviving infantry school and airborne school, I was becoming more confident, as well as being more arrogant about my capabilities. In my mind, I was indestructible.

"Take a seat at the table," said SFC Bailey.

"Yes, Sergeant."

I moved to the empty chair at the table where the other seven volunteers were already seated. In front of us, on top of the desk, were packets several pages thick. The young NCO who told me to wait in the hallway now stood at the end of the table closest to the platoon sergeant (PSG) and began to explain the instructions for the test.

"My name is SGT Howerton and I'll be in charge of the Scout selection process for the first week. In front of you is a packet consisting of eighty-two multiple choice and fill-in-the-blank questions that you will have to answer. You will be given thirty minutes to answer the questions in the packet. Once you are done, give me your packet and wait outside in the hallway by the Scout emblem on the wall. Does anyone have any questions?"

No one had questions.

"The test will begin in five, four, three, two, and one. Begin."

One after another, we finished the exam and turned in our packet to SGT Howerton. I was the last one to finish. I was new to the Army and the test consisted of questions relating to basic and advanced infantry and reconnaissance tactics I was not familiar with. The Scout platoon normally takes more experienced paratroopers, so after the test I had a feeling I was going to be sent back to B Co. We were told to wait in the hallway for the results.

After twenty minutes, SGT Howerton came out of the office and told everyone to gather around him. "Alright, good job, everyone. The test was only meant to measure your tactical knowledge so that we know, if you make it through the remaining two weeks of this selection process, what things we need to focus on to bring you up to speed."

I couldn't believe it. *God must want me to be a Scout*, I thought to myself, *because everything seems to be working out in my favor.*

Howerton continued, "Now, what I need you to do is for you to line up facing the Scout emblem, and I need you to recite the Ranger Creed out loud for me. Who here knows the Ranger Creed?"

I thought back to my days on Sand Hill when my battle buddy, Elijah, and I studied and learned the Ranger Creed. Elijah wanted to be prepared for the hell that is the Ranger Indoctrination Program.

"I know the Ranger Creed," I said, raising my hand and assuming I now had some type of advantage over the other volunteers.

"That's great, Arroyo, so why don't you begin by reciting the first stanza of the Ranger Creed."

Howerton looked to be no older than twenty-one years of age. He had blue eyes and was built like a triathlete. He had a calm and friendly demeanor that made me feel at ease around him as if Howerton was not the type of NCO to yell at a lower-ranking soldier. I imagined he would sit down with the troubled soldier and mentor him through one-on-one coaching.

The Ranger Creed consists of six stanzas beginning with each letter of the word "RANGER." Every Scout was required to learn the creed and to be able to recite it out loud. I began the first stanza of the creed loudly and confidently.

"Recognizing that I volunteered as a Ranger, fully knowing the hazards of my chosen profession, I will always endeavor to uphold the prestige, honor, and high esprit de corps of the Rangers!"

A deep sense of pride came over me as I managed to recite the first stanza of the creed without stopping.

Surely Howerton will be impressed, I thought to myself as I stood at attention, my head held high. But something changed about Howerton's demeanor once I finished the first stanza of the creed. He was no longer calm. He suddenly looked like a madman.

"What the f--- was that, Arroyo?!" he shouted as his white face flushed red. "You said you knew the proper way to recite the Ranger Creed and you lied to me! Now you, and all your wannabee Scout buddies, will suffer for your mistake! So, start pushing!"

We dropped to the floor and grabbed some tiles and began to do push-ups while Howerton continued to yell at us.

"The proper way to recite the creed is: 'First stanza of the Ranger Creed, repeat after me,' and it is then followed by the first stanza, naturally pausing during the reciting of the creed, so that your fellow wannabee Scouts can repeat what you just said! You're f------ embarrassing!"

Howerton was beyond irate and, for the next two hours, we did push-ups, lunges, burpees, and more. We did push-ups until we reached muscle failure and then we were ordered to lie on our backs and perform flutter kicks.

After listening to Howerton shouting at us, about six members of the Scout platoon came out of their barracks rooms and stood along the walls of the hallway watching us getting smoked. They watched in amusement as we were being ordered to duck walk from one end of the hallway to the other, and back. The hallway was about fifty meters long. One team leader, SSG Johnson, began offering technical advice to me to ensure I performed the duck walking exercise properly.

"Hey, Private, it helps if you quack when you do the exercise so that you can become one with the duck." The Scout platoon members all cracked up after hearing SSG Johnson's comment, and began to shout in unison "quack, quack, quack, quack!"

Those guys were sergeants and staff sergeants who endured far greater physical and psychological torment than what I was currently experiencing. Some of them graduated from some of the toughest schools the Army has to offer, like the Army Sniper School, the Long-Range Surveillance Leaders Course, and Sapper school. They, and Howerton, had no pity for us Scout candidates as they watched us duck walk from one end of the hallway and back.

The exercises continued. Then after one hour of cheering on the Scout wannabees, SSG Johnson decided eating popcorn would make the show more entertaining. He went into the Scout platoon office, where the microwave was located, and popped some corn. He was not greedy by any means, and he shared it with his fellow Scouts and even offered me some but, because eating food while working out is known to be a horrible mix, I respectfully declined his offer. After two hours one candidate approached SGT Howerton and said, "I hurt my knee in Special Forces Selection and I don't think that I should continue. Maybe I should go back to my unit and let it heal before I return."

All the Scouts in the hallway burst out in laughter. There was zero sympathy for anyone who quit, and especially for anyone who tried to use an injury as an excuse. SGT Howerton transformed himself back to being the calm and friendly guy he'd previously pretended to be, and he sympathized with the candidate.

"That's too bad, dude. I was really hoping that you would make it. Oh well, I guess you'll have to go back to your unit and hopefully you can tryout again soon." And with that, the candidate was dismissed, and the moment he walked out of the third floor every Scout in the hallway, including SGT Howerton, began to burst into laughter.

Watching the other paratrooper quit just made me more motivated. There was something about watching him break down and quit that fueled the fire inside me. I vowed to continue, regardless what happened next.

Two hours passed, and it was lunchtime. We were ordered to stop exercising and to report back to the Scout platoon office in two hours. After being relieved, I headed to the latrine and grabbed hold of a sink and then proceeded to puke my guts out. Every Scout in the hallway burst out in laughter and SGT Howerton entered the latrine to check on me.

"Are you alright?"

"Yes, Sergeant," I replied while spitting vomit out of my mouth.

"Finish up here and get some food in your stomach. Two hours should be enough time to eat and rest so that you have all the energy you're gonna need for the rest of the day, because I'm not gonna stop smoking your ass. So, get food and drink water, but if you want to quit then tell me now so that I'm not waiting on you to smoke you later."

I turned and looked at SGT Howerton with the same arrogant smirk I gave Lt. Z earlier and said, "I'll see you in two hours, Sergeant."

I stumbled out of the latrine, passing by every Scout in the hallway who was sure I would quit, and then headed to the chow hall for a quick refuel before the next round. Two hours later, I was back in the hallway, face down, doing push-ups, watching my reflection on the highly waxed tile floor turning into a blur from sweat dripping from me.

For the next five days, I endured that same repeated exercise torment, while learning all the tactical knowledge I was tested on, to the point where I was able to recite aloud, from memory, all the names of the Medal of Honor recipients of the 82nd Airborne Division, the infantry battle drills taught in basic training, various weapon system nomenclatures, the three types of reconnaissance missions, the eight troop-leading procedures, how to give an operations order, and the calculations for range estimation using the M-24 sniper rifle.

Most importantly, I mastered the proper way of reciting the Ranger Creed. Of the eight men who showed up for tryouts on that first day, only five remained. The first week of Scout tryouts came and went, and now we were headed into the wilderness of North Carolina, to train as members of a recon team, so the team leaders could evaluate each one of us and decide whether we were a good fit for the platoon.

It was a long, hellish week, but it was finally Friday and I was looking forward to getting some rest during the weekend. However, we couldn't leave without doing one last thing. We were ordered by SGT Howerton to line up facing the Scout emblem and recite the Ranger Creed. There are six stanzas to the Ranger Creed and, since there were only five Scout candidates left, it meant I had to recite the first and the last stanzas myself. All the Scouts stood in the hallway with a look that said, "You better not f--- this up!" Howerton propped open the door to the stairs because he wanted everyone in the building to hear.

"Let me hear the creed!" commanded SFC Bailey, so I began to sound off the first stanza as loud as I could, and the rest followed.

We recited the Ranger Creed at the top of our lungs and ended with a loud and thunderous "Rangers Lead the Way!" With that, we were dismissed until Monday morning at 0530, when we would venture out into the wilderness to prove our worth as part of a reconnaissance team.

It seemed like it only took thirty seconds for everyone to disappear for the weekend. Since I was a new soldier and recently moved in from the 1st Platoon barracks, I decided to stay in the barracks and organize my room and prepare my equipment for next week's field training exercise. As I was organizing everything, someone began to pound at my barracks room door. The first thing that came to my mind was I was going to be tested by the Scout platoon members and would not be allowed to rest the entire weekend. *No way! This sucks!* I fumed.

I opened the door to see SGT Birchfield, shirtless, wearing his BDU bottoms, his boots untied, and holding a beer.

"Yes, Sergeant?" I answered while standing at parade rest.

"Dude, relax. It's the weekend, bruh. It's time to get drunk!"

SGT Birchfield was tall, muscular, and had a tribal-style tattoo covering his left arm. He was only months away from the end of his four-year Army contract. After graduating from Ranger School, Sniper

School, the Long-Range Reconnaissance Surveillance Leaders Course, and just returning from a combat deployment to Afghanistan, he was no longer interested in being a "good soldier." He was a native of Bakersfield, California, and was more interested in girls, alcohol, and . . . girls.

"Dude, I saw the s--t you went through this week. I'm not gonna lie, dude, it was funny watching you throw up but—do you have any beer?" SGT Birchfield spoke with a California style I was familiar with.

"Sergeant, I'm eighteen years old and I can't buy beer so, no, I don't have any." I was still standing at parade rest.

"Dude, relax, bruh! Call me Max, dude. Let me bring some beer from my room. I'll be right back."

Max walked down the hall to his room and returned with two Dos Equis beers.

"Here, man, have one." I took the beer, opened it, and took a swig.

"Thanks, Max."

"No problem, dude . . . so where you from?"

"I'm from a small city in California called Bell Gardens." I was trying not to become too comfortable, since earlier SGT Howerton, who initially appeared to be a nice guy, turned into a total disciplinarian and made me vomit.

"Dude, I really don't care about this army s--t anymore and I'm over it but let me give you a word of advice to help you survive the years to come."

I was listening intently and expecting a long lecture, assuming Max would share some of his most intense combat experiences and the lessons he learned while surviving in the wilderness as a Scout team leader.

"What's your advice, Max?"

Max looked me right in the eyes with a stare fortifying the seriousness of what he was about to say.

"Don't be 'that guy'."

"What?" I expected a lengthier piece of advice from Max.

"Yeah dude, don't be 'that guy'."

"What guy?"

"You know when someone has f----- up and everyone wants to know who that guy is?"

"Yeah."

"Well, don't be 'that guy'."

With those words of wisdom, Sergeant Max Birchfield turned toward his room and walked away. A few weeks later, Max completed his time in service and was honorably discharged. He returned to California and was killed in a homicide.

Chapter Eight

The Hunted

I FELT THE propellers of the UH-60 Blackhawk helicopter cutting through the night air, and their vibration only added to my growing anxiety. It was approximately 2200 hours and the dark sky offered little visibility for the six of us on board, as the chopper traveled low to the ground to avoid being detected by the "enemy." The sound of the twin engines and the vibration of the propellers were magnified by the G-forces created by the very low altitude flight course taken by the pilot, exploiting valleys and folds in the terrain as he made his way to the Spivey Landing Zone.

"One minute!" shouted the copilot and everyone on board echoed the advisory. My heart was racing, and I became self-conscious about looking nervous as I noted the calm demeanor of the veteran Scouts. To them it was just a training exercise that would probably wind up being just another "suck fest" in the books. They were used to being inserted deep behind enemy lines in Afghanistan on missions to confirm or deny enemy activity.

"Thirty seconds!" With this everyone began to lean slightly forward in their seats and check their weapons. The shadows of the tree line became visible as the helicopter descended to the LZ. Once the helicopter touched down, we rapidly unfastened our three-point seat belts and exited the Blackhawk from its two doors and then dove to the ground in the prone position. Once we were all out, the helicopter ascended and disappeared into the night sky. Our Scout Team 3 simultaneously rose to our feet and moved off the LZ and into the cover of the wilderness.

For the next five days I carried out reconnaissance training operations in the wilderness of Fort Bragg, North Carolina, as part of the Scout platoon, Team 3—call sign Hawk 3. The Scout platoon consisted of three Scout teams, and each Scout team had six men, and a headquarters element consisting of the PSG, the platoon leader (PL), a radio telephone operator (RTO), and a medic.

For the training exercise, our teams were tasked with conducting zone, area, and route reconnaissance missions in and around what was deemed as being a drug lord's area of operations. Our mission was to provide the 1st Battalion, 505th Parachute Infantry Regiment with intelligence confirming or denying the presence of drug and weapons trafficking. If possible, we would also locate the drug lord. To succeed in our mission, we would have to remain undetected while infiltrating the areas of interest. And we had to do so while often being no more than an arm's length way from enemy personnel. The task was difficult, and it was not going to be made any easier. The next five days were an introduction to a world of stealth and stalking I was not taught in basic training.

For this training exercise, the headquarters element also served as the opposition force (OPFOR) and hunted our three Scout teams while we operated in the area. The PSG, the PL, the RTO, and even the medic, would be tracking our three teams through the wilderness in hopes of compromising our positions. The compromised team would have to perform escape and evasion (E&E) maneuvers to tactically move out of the area of operations, while being fired upon and hunted day and night by the OPFOR, to avoid being captured by the enemy. Meanwhile, our teams were being evaluated based on our performance, with each team leader and NCO. CSM Lambert expected these evaluation reports would help him determine whom he wanted to remain a leader in the Scouts, and whom he wanted removed and sent back to the "line platoon" (airborne infantry platoon) and replaced.

The Scouts wanted only the best men for the job, and the difficulty of being hunted by the headquarters element was only the beginning. Lt. Z happened to have a good friend in the 82nd Airborne Aviation Regiment who was an OH-58 Kiowa helicopter pilot. The Kiowa helicopter was equipped with a state-of-the-art mast mounted sight (MMS) gyro-stabilized vision system that looked like a giant basketball on top of the rotors. The Kiowa was also equipped with a thermal imaging system (TIS) and a laser range finder (LRF) which enabled it to detect vehicles, tanks, and—for the next five days—Scout platoon paratroopers.

From the air and on land, we were being tracked by the enemy while moving to our objectives. We were given a grace period of one hour from the time the helicopter insertion was completed before the OPFOR and the Kiowa gave chase. The clock was ticking for our team and the difficult task of navigating through the woods at a fast pace, while remaining undetected, would prove to be difficult.

After the helicopter left, we made our way into the wilderness. Once our team reached the wood line, we took a knee for five minutes to stop, look, listen and smell (SLLS), which allowed each of us to become familiar with the operational environment. This would help us distinguish between the natural and unnatural, with the unnatural being enemy activity. Once everyone was familiar with the environment, we began to make our way toward the first objective. It was a five-mile movement through the wilderness, made ever more difficult by the rocky terrain and the sixty pounds of equipment each of us carried.

Leading the team was SSG David McGillivray (Mac). He was an American of Scottish descent with blond hair with a dash of red. He was a burly man whose appearance was intimidating. He wasn't especially tall, but his V-shaped torso and broad muscular shoulders, coupled with his no-nonsense demeanor, gave him the commanding presence of a leader. McGillivray's field craft, intelligence, and experience personified leadership. A graduate of Army Ranger School, Special Forces Selection, and Survival Evasion Resistance and Escape School, Mac was the epitome of the type of leader the Scout platoon was looking for.

I had only indirectly interacted with Mac before this point. He laughed after he called me a "beaner" while doing strenuous physical exercises in the Scout platoon hallway. So I didn't know what to expect from SSG Mac out in the field, but I guessed it might be a bad experience.

We walked five miles under the cover of darkness to the objective rally point (ORP) and stopped to kneel, in circular formation, with each member facing out and away from one another. We were approximately one hundred fifty meters away from our first objective, which was a suspected enemy safe house.

The senior Scout observer and the Scout observer left their rucksacks at the ORP and donned their ghillie suits (special camouflage suits covered with vegetation) so they could move in closer to the suspected safe house. There they would take pictures and draw sketches of the objective, while also noting how many enemy personnel there were, and what type of firearms and equipment they carried. The Scouts carrying out the recon were SGT Mish and SPC Dunaway. They also donned ghillie suits and began to assist each other by putting leaves on the camouflage and burlap material of their suits. As they moved away from our team and toward the objective, I saw how they became indistinguishable from the surrounding natural vegetation.

It was now 0100 hours. While Dunaway and Mish were completing their recon, the sound of rotors broke the silence of the night. Off in the distance we saw the Kiowa helicopter flying in a circular pattern moving ever closer to our position. It was on the hunt for us and getting closer. The ORP would not offer us enough cover to avoid being detected by the advanced optics of the roving bird. Mac knew he had to move our team, but there was a problem. The two Scouts conducting their surveillance weren't back yet, and moving from the ORP could cause a break in contact, separating our team. That would result in the two men being compromised and hunted.

The sound of the helicopter moved closer, and we started to worry. Mac asked me to communicate the situation to the two Scouts on the objective, using the Icom radio, but they weren't answering. In less than a minute the Kiowa would be flying over us and we had to move. Mac gave the order for us to get our gear and Dunaway and Mish's gear and then move away from the objective and into a mosquito-infested swamp providing enough cover with its thick brush to avoid detection. Our team geared up and I grabbed SGT Mish's rucksack and prepared to move.

With the helicopter close to our position, we had to assume the OPFOR was moving close too, so we headed for the swamp. And now the helicopter was getting close, almost overhead. But now fifty meters away, Mac suddenly stopped and pointed his weapon which was the sign to alert the rest of the team of an immediate threat, so we could prepare to engage. We made a sudden halt mid-stride, pointed our weapons at a target we could not see and prepared to fire.

"Friendly!" shouted the silhouette in the brush. "Come out!" replied Mac. It was Mish and Dunaway. The team was complete, and we all made a run for it.

We made it to the swamp and jumped right in, neck deep and covered with swamp grass. The resident mosquitos wasted no time making a meal out of us, but there was nothing I or my team could do. The helicopter was overhead and flashing an infrared laser at anything remotely resembling a Scout in the woods. We were still as tree trunks as we tried to ignore the onslaught of mosquito bites. After a minute that seemed like an eternity, of loitering in the airspace over our team, the Kiowa departed and continued its search for Scouts in the surrounding area. We survived our first encounter against the Kiowa, but the week had just begun.

"Hawk 3 Romeo, this is Hawk 7, over." The voice of SFC Bailey came over the radio. He wanted to know the grid location of our team so he could link up with us to evaluate our team's performance, and SSG Mac's performance as well. Our Scout team was given a location to rendezvous with Hawk 7 who was three hundred meters away.

We got out of the swamp and began making the trek while brushing off all the remaining mosquitoes that were still sucking blood from our skulls. When we arrived at the grid location, we saw SFC Bailey wearing BDUs, jungle boots, LBE, and a boonie hat, standing by a Humvee with the headquarters RTO, SPC Cook, at the wheel. SSG Mac made his way to Hawk 7 as the rest of us sat back in the woods, leaning on our ruck sacks—"rucksack-flopped"—and waited for orders.

SFC Bailey informed SSG Mac that he would follow our team while coordinating the OPFOR to harass us during movement. That way we could practice our fighting tactics as a team in a simulated combat environment, but he would also use pyrotechnics (simulation grenades and artillery) to add more chaos to our assignment. After being briefed of the oncoming mission, SSG Mac walked back toward the rest of us, and he rucksack-flopped too.

"Well, this is gonna suck." Mac's voice offered no enthusiasm for us as we sat next to him waiting to hear the details of the next mission. SSG Mac—call sign Hawk 3—passed on the information. "Our mission is to make our way to a suspected enemy camp where it is believed that the enemy may have a weapons cache. We're supposed to locate the weapons cache and provide a ten-digit grid location to the cache so that an air weapons team can destroy it."

He continued, "Keep your eyes open for OPFOR, because Sergeant · Bailey is gonna be callin' 'em to get us when we least expect it, so prepare for the worst. Any questions?"

No one had any questions, so SSG Mac gave us an eight-digit grid to our location and then showed us exactly where we were on the map. I took note of this and marked it with a blue marker on my laminated map, with a single dot. We got up and began to move out.

The sun was up, and day two was underway. After thirty minutes of making our way to the suspected enemy safe house, SFC Bailey disappeared into the wilderness. We didn't talk while on patrol, to prevent being detected. Instead, we used hand and arm signals to communicate. We kept our heads on a swivel and constantly tried to identify any threat in the surrounding environment, while also making periodic eye contact with each other so any message needing to be shared could be disseminated. We moved in single file with five meters between each Scout, and I was the third in file order from the point man, SSG Mac. I looked behind me and made eye contact with SGT Mish who then pointed at his eyes and then pointed into the woods.

I looked and saw SFC Bailey. Once I made eye contact with the man in front of him, SGT Decker, I attempted to pass on the message, but I was interrupted by a large explosion. *Boom!*

The concussion of the blast shook up our entire team as we began to take enemy machine gun fire from a bunker at three o'clock. We all dropped to the ground while returning fire in the direction of the enemy. "Three o'clock, one hundred meters, enemy bunker!" I shouted at the top of my lungs hoping my teammates would hear it over the chaos; everyone echoed the command. Within seconds our trek turned into chaos. *Boom! Boom! Boom!* The explosions increased as SFC Bailey was pulling pin after pin from his simulation artillery grenades. Being in a small recon team means we are not able to sustain a gunfight for long, the way an infantry platoon could. Our best option when in contact with the enemy is to break contact and move away from the enemy as fast as possible.

"Smoke!" yelled SSG Mac, and he and I tossed smoke grenades at the direction of the enemy bunker to limit their visibility and begin to maneuver out of the area. A large white cloud created a visual barrier between us and the enemy, so we began to move using the center peel. Each one of us was engaging the enemy. And with the smoke barrier in full effect, SSG Mac stopped firing, jumped up to his feet, and—before bounding back and away from the enemy—he tapped SGT Decker on his shoulder to let him know he was the next person who needed to bound back.

Once each man finished bounding away from the enemy for about ten meters, they would then stop behind cover and concealment and begin to re-engage the enemy. One by one we jumped up, tapped the man next to us, and began to bound back. We did this until we were at a safe enough distance from the enemy and able to regroup, check each other for injuries, check our equipment, then move back toward the objective by taking an alternate route. We repeated the bounding maneuver about four times before we gathered ourselves and moved away from the area in a file formation. "Good job, guys," said SFC Bailey, who appeared from out of the wilderness. He ordered SSG Mac to continue to the objective and we began our journey once more.

It was 1200 hours and the temperature was on a steady rise. The 98-degree temperature with 90 percent humidity, topped with the thick North Carolina brush and sixty pounds of equipment we were carrying made for a horrible day. We finally found our way to the ORP, and this time it was SGT Mish and I who donned our ghillie suits and carried out the recon of the suspected enemy camp and weapons cache.

Prior to coming out to the field, SGT Howerton taught me how to make a ghillie suit and the proper way to stalk an enemy position and carry out a recon operation. But that took place outside the barracks and mostly in a class environment. Today I was going to have to jump into the "hot seat" and prove to my teammates I had the discipline and ability to be a member of this elusive platoon.

When Mish and I finished putting foliage on each other's ghillie suits, Mac signaled for me to make my way over to him. *He's probably gonna tell me something stupid and insult me*, I thought as I moved toward Mac, who was at the center of the ORP's circle formation.

"Hey, little buddy," began Mac, to my surprise, "I know you can do this. Stay low, move slow, and do your best." I was surprised. It seemed SSG Mac was a whole other person in the field. He was not a garrison soldier like many in the Army who loved wearing their starched uniforms and spit-shined boots, all while quoting the Army's uniform standards straight out of the AR 670-1 (Wear and Appearance of Army Uniforms and Insignia) to other soldiers. Instead, SSG Mac hated being in garrison and he thrived out in the wilderness and in combat. He was most comfortable and happiest in the "suck."

SGT Mish and I moved out toward the objective. We walked slow and stayed low to avoid detection. Once we had "eyes on" the objective, Mish instructed me to gather information moving counterclockwise from our position and Mish would move clockwise, and then we would meet at the opposite end of our current position, then make our way back to the ORP.

When conducting a recon, it was important for us to avoid walking parallel to the objective. That was because the human eye is able to pick up movement easier this way than it can when an object is moving directly toward it. To prevent being detected, we moved in a cloverleaf pattern by walking straight toward the objective, taking pictures, and drawing sketches and then moving backward, directly away from the objective. Once out of sight from the objective, we would move clockwise or counterclockwise as we determined, and repeat.

I was on my second loop on the objective, drew sketches, and took pictures using a digital camera. I could see our "enemies"—SPC Cook and the medic—dressed in desert uniforms attempting to locate us. They knew we were watching them. I moved toward the objective by lying flat on my stomach with my left ear down on the ground while creeping forward in a sniper crawl. I moved as slowly as a slug and often froze when SPC Cook or the medic stopped to look out of the second-story window facing my location. It often seemed like Cook or the medic spotted me as I lay there looking directly at them, with them staring right back at me, for minutes on end, but were unable to distinguish me from the surrounding environment. Reconnaissance is a job requiring patient men who push the limits of their own safety and move close enough to the enemy, without being detected.

Mish and I finished our final loop and met at the twelve o'clock of the objective and began to head back to the ORP. We maintained radio silence on our Icom's to avoid any noise that could give away our location, so Mish and I turned on our radios and let SGT Kline know we were heading back to the ORP. It took us about an hour to gather all the necessary intelligence, and Mish happened to find the suspected weapons cache on the objective.

When we arrived back at the ORP, we handed over our sketches and cameras to SGT Kline who called Hawk 6 (Lt. "Z") and reported all the information gathered on the objective. Every bit of information was important: everything from the clothes and boots the enemy wore, to the type of weapons they carried, the supplies they had and the amount of food and water they managed to keep available. Even their facial and physical appearance was important as it could reveal their morale and their level of discipline.

Once the recon was complete it was about 1400 hours and we received our next mission over the radio. Hawk 6 ordered Team 3 to set up a "belly hide" overlooking a certain strip of highway. It was believed the drug cartels were moving many weapons and drugs to the area of operations, and each Scout team was assigned a portion of the highway to watch. Each team was given a left and right limit of the portion of highway they were to observe. SSG Mac then briefed everyone on the mission, and after receiving information, we moved out to our next mission.

A belly hide is an underground hiding position large enough for at least two people, depending on the operation. Our six-man team would be split into three two-man teams with two of us per hide site. I was partnered with SGT Decker and we worked fast to build our belly hide using our portable excavation tool (E-Tool), digging a hole deep enough for the two of us. The belly hide had to be deep enough for us and our rucksacks. It also had to be deep enough so when we laid down on our bellies, we were below ground level. After digging the hole, we used fallen branches from the surrounding area to lay across the top of the hole and draped our woodland camouflage ponchos over the branches. Then we gathered leaves and foliage to cover the poncho liner and branches, with the intent of making the hide sight blend in with the surrounding environment, while remaining durable enough to withstand someone walking over it.

To avoid detection, we built it in a heavily wooded area people would most likely avoid traveling through. From the outside, the belly hide appeared level with the earth around it. To the front of the hide, facing the objective, we made two small three inch in diameter ports by separating the foliage to allow us to see the road. To the rear of the belly hide were two holes on each corner to allow for escape, but while we occupied the hide, we covered the holes with leaves and pine needles to avoid giving away our location.

Once it was ready, we crawled inside, belly first. We lay down with our rucksacks by our feet to the rear of the hide. We covered the rear entrances of the hide and began watching the road. Our mission for the next three hours was to watch the road and count how many military vehicles drove by our location. Twenty minutes into the mission I began to crash. It had been almost twenty-four hours since my last meal and I expended thousands of calories carrying all my gear and crawling for hours. I could hear SGT Decker's stomach growling as we lay flat on our bellies while fighting the urge to sleep. We were not allowed to pack any food as Lt. Z instructed us before the training exercise that he would provide us with all of the food we would need to survive. We had two and a half hours left of observation and SGT Decker knew for us to accomplish our mission we needed a rest plan.

We watched the road in twenty-minute shifts so we could take turns resting our eyes, but not sleeping. And truthfully, I was so hungry I couldn't have slept if I'd wanted to. I thought of my mom's cooking and how my family back home in California had a delicious dinner last night, followed by watching television while wearing comfortable clothes and sitting on a couch. I wished for home, in that ugly one-bedroom house I wanted to leave so bad as a kid. But now, there was nothing I could do but wipe the drool from my mouth and continue the mission. Three horrible hours passed, and it was 1730. The sun was beginning to set, and we received the call to abandon the belly hide. We made our way back to the ORP where all three Scout teams were waiting.

When I arrived, SFC Bailey and Lt. Z were already there along with the headquarters element. The prevailing thought on everyone's mind was food. As the rest of the platoon gathered at the ORP, all we could talk about was how we wanted to eat. Lt. Z heard us and, once everyone was accounted for, Lt. Z gave us our next mission: "Each team is tasked with finding a cache. In these caches is resupply equipment such as food, ammunition, and medical supplies."

"You had me at food," said SSG Johnson, Team 2 leader, and we all cracked up. Lt. Z then continued, "The sun is setting, so it behooves you to move with a purpose so that you can take advantage of the light to help you on your search. If you don't find your respective cache, then you will not be offered an opportunity to eat until we do this again in the next twenty-four hours. Good luck!"

SFC Bailey then read aloud the location to each team's cache, and we began to move out in a hurry. But before we did, Lt. Z had one more announcement to make. "Oh, hey guys! I almost forgot. The Kiowa is on station and making its way over here. You will be hunted during this event and if you are found before you find your meal, you're f---ed!" Now everyone began to walk at a pace just a little slower than running. It was important we moved with a purpose to beat the setting sun because finding a buried box in the wilderness of Fort Bragg was a lot easier with the help of the sun. And now, with the helicopter on its way, time was already running out.

Each team had their own cache in proximity of the others, so the team leaders came up with a plan. First, each team would look for their own cache, and then once a team found their cache, they would meet up with the teams who had not found theirs to help them. Each team was working together in the limited visibility of dusk and yet they all had trouble finding their own cache. It was now dark, and twenty minutes passed when over the radio Hawk 1 announced they found their cache. SSG Mac took the team to the area where the cache was hidden and ordered the team to work in pairs and search the area in a zigzag pattern. I was paired with SGT Decker and we moved with a sense of urgency, driven by our hunger.

We were wearing (PVS-14) night vision goggles connected to what we called "skull crushers," which were headbands with a chin strap and a hard polymer port on the forehead where we could mount our night vision. SGT Decker noticed a tree trunk with an abnormal amount of loose dirt beneath it. We approached it with caution, and we were careful not to rush and start digging around it for fear that it could just be an ant hill. But upon further inspection, SGT Decker kicked the tree trunk over, revealing a box of MREs. *FOOD!* I didn't shout it out loud, but I wanted to. We removed the loose dirt from on top of the MRE box and pulled the box out of the hole.

After removing the box, we discovered extra content. It was a burlap sandbag filled with gravel rather than sand and in big red letters the words "Medical Supplies" was written on it. We pulled the bag out and we were both surprised at how heavy the bag was. "It must be like twenty-five pounds," said SGT Decker. I slung my weapon behind me and picked up the bag, placing it over my left shoulder while SGT Decker carried the box of food. SGT Decker notified the rest of the team with his Icom radio and by this time all the other teams had found their food and "medical supplies," and moved out of the area.

We left the cache area in search of a safe place providing enough cover for us to stop and eat our meal while avoiding being detected by the Kiowa helicopter, whose rotors could be heard approaching our position. SSG Mac made a quick halt, and we discussed our options. We looked at our maps and concluded that moving to the nearest swamp was our best chance for avoiding detection. Although no one had exactly enjoyed the previous mosquito-infested swamp experience, we knew it was the best course of action. Being a grunt is not a glamorous job, and for us Scouts, whose job it is to move ahead of the infantry battalion to gather information while remaining undetected, it required being cold, wet, and miserable more often than most other military occupations. Once again, we found ourselves running from the Kiowa which was circling the cache area where we were moments earlier.

The Kiowa began its search pattern circling over our cache site while our team hurried toward the swamp. We were walking through tall grass and thick mud while the mosquitoes ate us alive. No amount of mosquito repellent was able to keep those monsters away but even if we had any we were not allowed to wear it because the smell could compromise our position.

Now angry because we wanted to eat, and wet because we'd been in a swamp, we rucksack-flopped in the tall grass just a few feet away from a stream of water. We remained silent and still as we all looked up at the sky and watched the helicopter circle our position, hoping we would not be compromised. After loitering the area overhead for a minute, the helicopter moved on to continue its hunt for the teams.

I breathed a sigh of relief and then we got up and moved out and away from the swamp. We finally got to eat our meal, and after such a long time without eating, we were all very disappointed. The one meal we were given was not enough and, although our stomachs stopped growling, we were all still hungry. After eating and changing our socks, we took turns sleeping. In total, we each slept about one hour before receiving our next mission over the radio.

We repeated this process each day until the end of the operation.

When that day finally rolled around, all the teams were ordered to meet up at a training site at a former Rockefeller family estate. Called the Overhill training area, it was purchased by the Army years before. It was noon on a Friday and the temperature was a crisp ninety degrees with eighty percent humidity. On our way to the Overhill location, it was announced the Kiowa was called off, along with the OPFOR, so we stopped being tactical and moved along a dirt road while talking to one another. I felt relieved after spending the last four days in the wilderness communicating with my teammates, for the most part, through hand and arm signals.

While walking along the road we had to stop several times to rest as SSG Mac felt it necessary to do so. SSG Mac took it upon himself to carry the twenty-five-pound bag of rocks and refused to allow anyone else to carry it. This meant he walked for many miles while carrying over 100 pounds. I didn't understand why Mac said no to anyone offering to carry it. I told him a few times, "Sergeant, I can carry it for a bit if you want."

"It's alright, little buddy," replied SSG Mac as he reached out with his arm so I could help him stand up.

The experience I shared with SSG Mac those five days out in the field was anything but what I expected. SSG Mac was a professional war-fighter who led from the front and who never asked his team to do anything that he wouldn't do. For him to have carried those extra pounds for such a long distance over the course of five days made me reconsider my opinion of him.

We walked approximately six miles before reaching the rendezvous point. We made our way down a fire break (a manmade trail in the woods meant to slow or stop the spread of a wildfire) surrounded by trees when there was a sudden break in the tree line, and we approached an open area beside a beautiful lake and old horse stables. There were several colonial-style homes in sight and parked in front of one white house with gray shutters were Lt. Z, SFC Bailey, SPC Cook, and the medic. We stopped and hid in the wood line where we could watch them.

"All call signs, this is Hawk 3 Romeo, over," SGT Kline said over the Icom radio so the HQ element could not overhear. "This is Hawk 1, over." "This is Hawk 2, over."

"All call signs, this is Hawk 3 Romeo. Does anyone have eyes on the HQ element?" All the teams took the same action and were also watching the HQ element.

After five days of torment while being hunted in the wilderness, the three Scout teams were not taking any chances at walking into an ambush or some other unpleasant surprise Lt. Z dreamed up. We observed every movement of the HQ element and watched for any signs of bad intentions. There were no red flags, so all the teams agreed over the radio to come out from the cover of the wood line and walked directly toward the HQ element.

"Oh, damn!" exclaimed Lt. Z and SFC Bailey when they saw all three Scout teams walk out from the wood line at the same time from three different locations. "Were you guys watching us?" asked the lieutenant in disbelief. "I am impressed! Great job, guys, but I feel weird knowing now that you were keeping an eye on me the whole time. I feel violated for some reason." He said it with a big smile from ear to ear.

He was proud of his platoon's performance and especially by the fact each team accomplished every mission while avoiding being detected by the OPFOR and the Kiowa helicopter. To celebrate, Lt. Z and SFC Bailey set up a BBQ grill they brought on their Humvee, along with some hamburger patties, potato chips, and sodas. It was 1600 hours of day five, and the torment that began Monday at 0400 for preparation, followed by the 2200 helicopter insertion, was now over.

"Index!" shouted Lt. Z to announce the official end of the training exercise. Every Scout lost twenty or more pounds over the last five days and were all ready for some hot chow. SPC Cook fired up the charcoal grill and everyone dropped all their equipment. SSG Mac was relieved to finally be able to remove the over 100 pounds he carried for three days.

While we relaxed and ate burgers next to a nice colonial setting overlooking the lake, we shared stories about being chased by the Kiowa and hiding in swamps. Someone from Team 1 said he was taking a dump in the woods when the Kiowa showed up. He had to "pinch it off" and run for it to join the rest of his team. We were laughing and having a good time when we saw Lt. Z pick up his MBITR.

"Venom One Three, this is Hawk 6, over." He was calling the Kiowa.

"Hawk 6, this is Venom One Three, over."

"We are at grid location . . ."

We started to panic. Was this a curveball? We all looked at each other and slowly moved closer to our gear. I was ready to put on my rucksack and run. I heard the propellers of the helicopter approaching but I couldn't see it. Lt. Z looked over at us and laughed.

"Hey relax, guys! Venom One Three is joining us for burgers!"

"Oh, man." I'd thought this was some sort of mind game. We laughed at each other but especially at SGT Howerton. He already had his rucksack on, and his weapon slung, with a soda in one hand and a burger in the other. But he just shrugged. "Hey, man, If I'm running into the woods, I'm taking some hot chow with me!"

The sound of the rotors grew stronger, and I could feel their vibration chopping in the wind. The Kiowa helicopter that had been hunting us emerged from the top of the wood line. The pilot had been flying low to the ground behind the tree line and once he located us using the advanced optics on the helicopter, he emerged and made himself known. He landed the helicopter on the dirt road just fifty meters away from the white colonial style home where we were hanging out. When the pilot and copilot got out, I didn't know whether we were going to shake their hands or beat the daylights out of them for chasing us these last few days.

"Alright, guys, please don't hurt me. I'm just a lowly helicopter pilot."

We laughed. But I'm sure he could tell we weren't comfortable around him and his copilot. Still that joke broke the tension.

"Who was the dude taking a dump by the swamp? I saw a guy running with his BDU bottoms halfway down his ass!"

After everyone had their fill of laughter and hamburgers, and the pilots flew off back to the 82nd Airborne Aviation hangar, Lt. Z ordered the entire platoon to take a knee in a horseshoe formation around him.

"Good job, everyone! I, Sergeant Bailey, and the rest of the HQ element, including the Kiowa, were hunting you and yet you got away. Each team accomplished the mission they were given and the drug lord, which was me, was spotted and killed by a Joint Direct Attack Munition (JDAM) Team 1 called in." He went on to say, "To all of the new guys, congratulations, welcome to the Scout platoon."

I felt a great sense of accomplishment. Up to that point, this was the toughest test of my military career. However, for the next six months, the training never stopped. Morning PT every day was a challenge and reciting the Ranger Creed and getting smoked in the barracks hallway continued.

Then, as time went on, our training took on a more urban setting. Saddam Hussein refused to allow weapons inspectors into his country, and rumors that we were going to war were spreading throughout the 82nd Airborne.

I was ready.

Chapter Nine

Love

AFTER THE SCOUT tryouts were over, I was back at the B Co. barracks on a Saturday morning, gathering my things. I was leaving those barracks and moving into the Scout platoon floor. I didn't have much stuff to move, since I was the new guy living off whatever I had in my duffel bags. As I packed my belongings, I reached for a folder holding my military documents including my certificate of completion from infantry and airborne school, and my orders to report to Fort Bragg. As I shoved the folder into my already overstuffed green duffel bag, a small piece of paper fell out. I stuffed the folder into the duffel bag and picked up the folded, one-inch square of paper. I opened it and saw the name Sarah and a phone number.

I met Sarah my senior year in high school, and I thought she was great. Just seeing her name on that scrap of paper reminded me of her beautiful brown hair and hazel-colored eyes. She had a sweet smile and a rocking hot body. I was debating with whether I should call her. I once asked her to be my girlfriend and she rejected me. At the time, she'd told me she doubted whether a relationship with me would work out because I was leaving for the Army. I was heartbroken when she said that, but for some reason I'd kept her number. And now there it was in my hand, and I had to make a choice: toss it or call her?

I stepped outside the barracks, pacing back and forth beside the pull-up bars, my cell phone in my hand. I punched in all the digits of her phone number, but didn't hit "send." I'm not sure what was holding me back. Maybe I thought it would be a waste of time, since she already rejected me, and anyway, maybe she was right. I was on the other side of the country in North Carolina, and she was in Bell Gardens enjoying her life without me. But after ten minutes of pacing back and forth and tightly clutching my phone, I unlocked the screen and hit send.

My heart was pounding in my chest as the phone rang. A part of me hoped she changed her number and the call wouldn't go through. I was nervous after the third ring and thought about hanging up.

"Hello?"

"Hey, may I speak with Sarah?"

"Fernando! Is that you?"

"Yeah, it's me."

"Oh my God, where are you? I've been worried about you."

"Really? I'm in North Carolina! So, you've been worried about me, huh?"

"Yeah, maybe just a little bit. Every time I see military stuff on the news, I think about you. I just want to know that you're safe. But honestly, I've been thinking a lot about you."

When I heard her say she was thinking about me, my heart starting racing so fast I thought she could probably hear it through the phone. *No way!* I thought to myself. *Stay cool, bro. Don't mess this up!*

"I've been thinking about you too. I would love to see you again."

"Fernando, I'm sorry if I hurt you when I said it wouldn't work out between us. I was afraid of having my heart broken because you're so far away. But I really like you and I want to see you."

"I'll be home in July; I would love to see you too."

"Yeah, I would really like that."

"Listen, I'm in the middle of moving my stuff to another building but it was great talking to you. I'm really glad that I made this phone call!"

"I'm glad you did too. Don't be a stranger! You better call me. I'll be waiting for you back home. I'm so excited! I can't wait to see you again!"

"I look forward to seeing you too. Take care."

"You too, soldier! You better call me."

"I will! I'll talk to you soon. Bye."

"Bye, Fernando."

When I hung up the phone, I felt like I'd just jumped out of a C-130. My adrenaline soared. I couldn't believe this girl was thinking about me. Had she really said she missed me? I couldn't believe I almost tossed that small square of paper in the trash!

Chapter Ten

Rumors of War

SCOUT TRAINING NEVER let up. Every morning I woke at 0500 to brush my teeth, shave, and clean my barracks room. By 0545 everyone in my platoon was in the hallway and all the new Scouts who weren't tabbed (Ranger School graduates) had to recite the Ranger Creed and get smoked. By 0630 we were doing PT as a platoon and SFC Bailey and Lt. Z took turns torturing us.

PT usually began with a two-mile sprint; we were running five-and-a-half-minute miles. We'd stop and do twenty-five eight-count bodybuilders, which are like burpees but with two push-ups. Then we rolled over on our backs and did flutter kicks, followed by another "sprint" but this time only one mile. Afterward we went back to the barracks, changed into our BDUs, with LBE and a dummy M-16 rifle, then ran over to the swimming pool for pool PT.

We jumped into the pool, and while treading water with our dummy rifle over our heads, we recited the Ranger Creed, followed by singing the 82nd Airborne song. Then we swam a few laps, about twenty-five meters, keeping our rifles out of the water. When we finished up at the pool, we ran back to the barracks (about half a mile) and mounted the pull-up bars. Once each Scout was on a bar, we did ten pull-ups, then hung free on the bar and recited the Ranger Creed. After pull-ups, with our arms smoked, we climbed ropes (just once) then headed back to the barracks. After morning PT, I usually had about forty-five minutes or less to shower, change into clean BDUs, and eat breakfast chow.

Following chow, we had classes where I learned many essential lessons taught by all the amazing NCOs (non-commissioned officers/sergeants) in my platoon: how to plan and execute an ambush, raid and recon operations; how to use the M-24 sniper rifle, Barret .50 caliber sniper rifle, range estimation, infiltration, and overwatch of known areas of interest, making urban hide sites, and combat lifesaver (medical training). If I was not learning sniper stuff, I was learning the use of various radio systems. I was taught how to use the high frequency radio (HF), tactical satellite, and the automated net control device (ANCD). We also practiced calling for mortar and artillery fire, and communicating with Apache Longbow helicopters and Kiowa helicopters.

One of the coolest experiences I had at a shooting range was training with the Army Special Forces (SF), better known as the Green Berets. Some of the SF 18 Bravo (weapons sergeant) course instructors from the John F. Kennedy Special Warfare Training Center invited us to train in the familiarization and use of Soviet weapons. That was literally a blast! Those SF guys were experts in the use of all sorts of weapons systems, so I had fun learning from the best. I got to fire the AK-47, SKS-45, RPG, and the ZU-23 anti-aircraft gun. The ZU-23 was amazing! It had two barrels that fired 23mm rounds. I sat and fired a few rounds into a mountain side. Amazing!

Training was challenging and sometimes fun, but we were also closely monitoring the situation in Iraq. Saddam Hussein was not allowing UN inspectors to enter his country to confirm he did not have weapons of mass destruction (WMDs). So the U.S. started building up troop presence in Kuwait, and the rumor was we, the 1-505 PIR, were going to go to war with Iraq.

Rumors of war in the 82nd Airborne are like gossip. Some staff NCO would tell another NCO what he heard a two-star general say to a colonel. Then some other NCO would say they heard "that colonel" say to his lieutenant colonel to "Get ready." Then, the gossip would eventually trickle down to the 1-505 PIR barracks, and everyone would get pumped up for war. The rumors would normally be false, and we would all be disappointed. But every now and then, they turned out to be true, and that was the moment we lived for.

When the invasion of Iraq started, at first my unit was left on the sidelines, watching troops fighting in Iraq on CNN like every other American. We were more than annoyed because we had a rotation in the 82nd known as Deployment Ready Force (DRF). The 82nd Airborne maintains a brigade-sized force (about 6,000 paratroopers) ready to deploy anywhere in the world within eighteen hours of notification. Our sister brigade, the 325th Airborne Infantry Regiment, was the current unit on DRF 1. My unit was on DRF 2, and we were set to assume DRF 1 in one month. If the invasion of Iraq happened during that time, we would have been first in line to deploy. But instead, the boys of 325 were deployed and were on the road to Baghdad.

One day after morning PT, I was eating breakfast in the chow hall while watching the invasion of Iraq on CNN when a breaking news story came in. A convoy of Army supply soldiers were ambushed after getting separated and lost and wandering into a city. The news report said one female soldier, named Jessica Lynch, was captured after she fought relentlessly against the enemy. The news reporter said Jessica fired her M-16 until her weapon jammed and she was shot and captured by the enemy. My heart sank when I heard the news, and I said a short prayer in my mind for Jessica. *Lord, protect her, wherever she is, and bring her home safe. Amen.*

My response was a lot different than that of combat veterans. The chow hall erupted with laughter as many paratroopers yelled, "It's called weapons maintenance, moron!" Others yelled, "Lies! That never happened!" No one was buying the story. Later it turned out she never fired a shot and the news media and the Pentagon made it all up.

A few weeks later, I watched on television as Jessica Lynch was carried onto a helicopter after being rescued by special operations forces. The "word on the street" (paratrooper gossip) was the 1st Ranger Battalion, SEAL Team 6 and Air Force Pararescue (PJs) carried out the mission to rescue Jessica. I was happy to know my buddy Elijah graduated from the Ranger Indoctrination Program and was a member of the 1st Ranger Battalion.

The invasion of Iraq was over. On May 1, 2003, President Bush declared the U.S. mission was accomplished. The war came and went without the men of the 1-505 PIR. We were all pretty bummed out about that. The new rumors were we wouldn't be needed in Iraq and, since things were slow in Afghanistan, we wouldn't go to Afghanistan either. I was disappointed. I enlisted to fight for America and now it seemed live fire exercises were the closest I would come to combat.

Then in July 2003 my unit was set to assume DRF 1 in August. And there were many restrictions during DRF 1. We couldn't travel more than one hour away from base, we had to have our cell phones with us at all times, and we had to sign out at the front desk of our company barracks, writing down where we were going and with whom. And since we were soon going to have many restrictions, we would have two weeks of leave before assuming DRF 1. And that meant I was finally going to see Sarah!

I kept in touch with her for the previous three months and we were looking forward to being together. I probably wasn't going to war, so being with Sarah was the best thing I had to look forward to. With my leave permission slip signed and my plane ticket in hand, my buddies and I carpooled to the Raleigh/Durham airport and boarded separate flights to our respective homes.

As I fastened my seatbelt, *Sarah, here I come!* was the foremost thought on my mind.

Chapter Eleven

The Rumors Were True

EVERYONE IN MY family stared at me like I was a different person. My mom looked me up and down while she touched my arms and my chest, feeling my muscles. *"Mijo, mira nomas que chulo te miras."* (Son, look just how handsome you are.)

I left home for the Army a scrawny 138-pound kid, and I returned a lean 150-pound paratrooper. I didn't realize how much my training changed me. My parents no longer saw me as a kid and my relatives, who said I wouldn't make it through infantry and airborne training, were all impressed.

I was happy to be home after such a long time of being away, but I had one thing on my mind—seeing Sarah. After I spent a few hours with my family, answering all their immediate questions about my training and my experience jumping out of a C-130, I stepped outside and called Sarah.

"Hey, it's me, what's up?"

"About time you called! You've kept me waiting for too long. I really want to see you."

"Well, I'm sorry. I'll pick you up in five minutes."

"Okay. Don't be late."

I was nervous. I trained to fight in combat and parachute out of airplanes, but I was about to see my high school sweetheart and that was a different story. I borrowed my brother's Jeep and drove just a few blocks to Sarah's house. Before I reached the front door she came out and walked toward me smiling. She whispered, "Hey, you," and we hugged. She looked me up and down and gave me another hug.

As I held her in my arms she whispered, "I'm so happy you're here. I missed you."

We went out every day for those two weeks. She showed me her college, we went to the beach several times, and we laughed a lot, enjoying our shared happiness every time we were together. We really hit it off.

Then, on the last day of my two-week leave, I received a call from SSG Mack.

"Hey, Arroyo, what are you up to? Eating tacos and hitting piñatas or something?"

"Ha! Negative, I'm out with my lady friend. Why? What's up?"

"Check it out! Apparently, Iraq is out of control and they want our unit to take care of it. There's a certain part of Iraq, somewhere around Baghdad, where Saddam's soldiers are leading an uprising. Enjoy your leave because we're going."

"Dang! All right, Sergeant!"

"Enjoy your tacos."

Sarah and I were walking on the shore in Long Beach, California, when I got the call and maybe my facial expressions gave it away. She could tell something was up. "So, who was that?"

"My team leader."

"What did he want?"

"He was just checking in on me."

"Was that it?"

"Yeah."

She looked at me like she knew I wasn't telling her everything. I just grabbed her hand and gently pulled her closer to my side as we walked on the sand. We watched the sun set that night and then we went to a movie. That was the night of our first kiss. As we watched the movie, Sarah gently put her hand on my chin and turned my head toward her. With her beautiful hazel eyes looking at me, she said, "What are you waiting for?" I slowly leaned into her and she leaned toward me. Our lips locked as our eyes closed. It was an amazing moment.

I held her hand as I drove her home that night and I parked in front of her house. I turned off the car and we kissed a little more. But then she looked at me with the same expression of concern on her face she had on the beach.

"There's something you're not telling me. What was that phone call about?"

I paused for a second as I caressed her hand with my thumb. I knew I had to tell her, but I didn't want to ruin our last night together.

"My team leader called to tell me that we're going to Iraq. I don't have a date yet, but it won't be long after I get back to Bragg."

Her eyes flooded and tears started rolling down her cheeks. I hugged her and told her everything was going to be okay, walked her home, and stepped inside to say goodbye to her family. Being a traditional Mexican family, I'd had to ask her father permission to date his daughter and that made her mother happy. Her family was good to me, pleased that Sarah and I were dating. When we walked through the door, her family knew something was wrong because they could see Sarah had been crying.

"*Mija, que tienes?*" Sarah's mom wanted to know what the matter was.

"Fernando is leaving."

"I know, but he's gonna visit soon."

"No, he's leaving for Iraq."

Sarah couldn't hold back her tears anymore. She hugged me and put her face on my chest as she cried. All I could do was hold her. Her mother also cried, and she hugged me as her daughter cried in my arms. After a few minutes, I had to go. I said goodbye to Sarah's family and Sarah walked me to the car.

"I'll be here. I will wait for you." And in true Mexican fashion, without skipping a beat, she said, "You better write to me!" as she slapped my shoulder.

"Dang, girl! Of course, I'm gonna write to you!"

"Well, you better!"

We both leaned in for one more kiss. I wanted to remember her fragrance and her smile and everything else about her. I said goodbye, slowly got into the car, and drove away.

I didn't know whether I would ever see her again.

Chapter Twelve

Compromised

MY PLATOON AND I arrived at the Baghdad International Airport and, after a week of acclimating to the heat, we were tasked with a mission. We received a report Iraqi insurgents were converging on an old Iraqi military base that night, looking for explosives.

Our mission was to insert into the Iraqi base and set up an observation point (OP) to confirm or deny these reports. If the reports were true and Iraqi insurgents were taking explosives, then we were to kill them. The difficult part about this mission was finding a building tall enough for us to set up our OP. The base was heavily bombed during the "Shock and Awe" campaign that kicked off the invasion, and very little was left of it. To make matters worse, it was believed the Iraqi army also used the base to house chemical weapons. But we were "reassured" there were no chemical weapons, based on a report (whatever that meant).

I prepped my gear for the mission, but I only carried the standard six 30-round magazine load, one extra radio battery for each radio (Icom, ASIP, and MBITR), 10 high explosive (HE) 40mm grenades for my 203 and two hand grenades. I tried my gear on and I was ready. We would be heading out on a patrol with B Co., 2nd Platoon, at 1200 hours. By 1700 hours we'd be dropped off outside the military base where we would locate an OP. Our tentative site was on the top floor of a narrow five-story warehouse in which missiles were probably launched or built. The satellite images (Google) showed multiple holes on the building walls, probably bomb damage.

It was going to be a long day and a long mission. Before leaving, I sat on my cot and said a prayer. "Lord, I pray that You would protect us as we go out and do our mission. I pray that You'll watch over our families back home and that You keep my mom and Sarah safe. In the name of our Lord, Jesus Christ, I pray, Amen."

That night, we headed for the Iraqi bomb factory. As predicted, the base was a disaster. It was a field of rubble and protruding rebar.

"Bravo Two Six, this is Hawk 3 Romeo, radio check, over." I wanted to make sure I had contact with the 2nd Platoon, PL (Bravo Two Six).

"Hawk 3 Romeo, this is Bravo Two Six, I read you Lima Charlie [loud and clear], over."

"That's a good, copy. Hawk 3 Romeo, out."

B Co. 2nd Platoon would serve as our Quick Reaction Force (QRF) so they circled the wagons in the open desert, about fifteen minutes away from our position. They were ready to help us if we ran into trouble.

When they dropped us off on the objective, I quickly took note of the five-story building we were supposed to use as our OP. Then Johnson and Mac spotted a building that was still intact and decided we should go check what was in it. We made our way into the concrete building. We stacked at the doorway, then entered to clear the building. We cleared our corners and maintained our sectors of fire, just like we were trained.

Then an odd smell entered my nose. It smelled like strong nail polish and I felt my eyes burning, like I was back in the tear gas chamber in training. Now everyone's eyes were burning, and we started coughing uncontrollably. Snot was dripping from my nose and I was dry heaving, along with everyone else. The news reports said there was no "smoking gun" chemical weapon in Iraq, but I'm pretty sure we inhaled something very similar.

We grabbed one another's sleeves, and pretty much dragged each other out of that building. We coughed for a few minutes while dry heaving, and made sure no one was left inside. Once everyone was accounted for, we found our way up the five-story missile silo–type warehouse. After all that, the walk up the stairs was brutal. I ditched a lot of my equipment but having inhaled some of that chemical made it hard for me to breathe, plus the stairs were steep, with the floors being taller than in a normal building—each floor was the equivalent of about three apartment floors back home.

Finally, we reached the fifth floor and used several of the large holes on the walls to observe the area. For 300 meters or so we could see nothing but rubble, and three two-story buildings, still standing. They were about the size of a two-bedroom home. PFC Rosetta and I watched the stairway and we made radio checks, making sure we had communication with the QRF. CPL McGuire had the Barrett M82A1 .50-caliber sniper rifle, and SGT Howerton and SSG Johnson had M-24 sniper rifles.

Rosetta and I were able to contact the QRF, but the transmission was received with a lot of static—broken and distorted. I pulled out my field expedient antenna which was made up of copper wire. It was connected to a metal clip on one end, and an antenna connector on the other. I hooked up the antenna connector to the radio, and the metal clip to a metal beam in the building. This turned our OP into a giant antenna, and when I called Bravo Two Six again, the transmission was perfect.

From 2000 hours to 0200, we observed the 300 meters of rubble with no activity. Mac and Johnson made the call to move our team into one of the two-story buildings. The building we were in was too full of holes to provide our team with cover during daylight hours. Sunrise was at about 0500 so we had to move. We packed our equipment and made our way down the stairs. We entered one of the two-story buildings and cleared it. Then Mac ordered a rest plan.

We were an eight-man team so two of us would stay awake for thirty minutes while the others slept. Every thirty minutes a new buddy team would take watch. Decker and I took the first shift, and I was exhausted. I struggled to keep my eyes open for those thirty minutes because the adrenaline had faded. I felt like I had to flex my forehead muscles just to keep my eyelids from closing. The thirty minutes passed, and we woke up the next shift. I did one more radio check with Bravo Two Six and, after they responded, I fell asleep.

There were two ways we would wake each other up. Our standard operating procedure (SOP) was to, first, shake someone until they awakened, which meant they needed to get up. The second was to squeeze the arm or leg of the Scout which meant "open your eyes and move slowly, because the enemy is approaching." I felt someone squeezing my left arm and heard them whisper, "Hey, little buddy, get your ass up."

It was Mac. I opened my eyes and saw him kneeling next to me. The sun was up, and I heard someone speaking in Arabic. I got up slowly and I noticed everyone in the team was kneeling. We were surrounded by about fifty Iraqi males. We peeked out the windows of the building and noticed those men were not armed. In fact, it was obvious they weren't after any explosives. They were after the rebar from the bomb-damaged buildings. All they wanted to do was recycle the metal to make money.

"Call Bravo Two Six and tell him we need to exfil [exfiltrate] ASAP." Mac was whispering as the sound of voices yelling in Arabic and hammers breaking concrete was growing louder. I called for the exfil and learned it would take about fifteen minutes before the QRF would arrive. We stayed quiet and out of sight as we waited patiently for our ride out of the situation.

We were on the second floor and we heard someone walking up the concrete stairs toward us. The doorway was in the right corner of the room, facing the stairway. We slowly moved to the left of the room, away from the doorway, with Decker and McGuire next to the doorway, ready to grab anyone who entered.

A young Iraqi male entered the room and, as soon as he set foot inside, Decker jumped up, placed his right hand on the Iraqi's mouth and his left hand behind his head. Decker pulled him down to the floor and McGuire used zip ties to handcuff him. With Mac's rifle pointed at his face, Decker placed his index finger over his own lips and gave the Iraqi the universal, "Shhh" so the young man wouldn't speak or cry out. The Iraqi was skinny, about twenty years old and he looked terrified. His eyes were wide open as McGuire tied a rag around his face to cover his mouth. Decker patted him down for weapons and then made the Iraqi kneel, facing the corner of the room.

"Where's Bravo Two Six?" Mac whispered to me. "Let them know that we are compromised."

I called Bravo Two Six and informed him of our dilemma.

"Five minutes out," I told Mac, staring at the young Iraqi. This was my first time seeing an Iraqi zip-tied and I couldn't believe I woke up to this.

We heard another voice calling from downstairs, in Arabic, "Muhammad?" He was looking for his buddy who was currently unavailable to respond. "Watch this guy," Decker whispered to me, so I pointed my rifle at the young Iraqi as Decker and McGuire took their positions for another take down. The second Iraqi stepped into the room, and Decker and McGuire gave him the same treatment. Once he was zip-tied, McGuire placed him in a different corner of the room.

I watched the first Iraqi while Rosetta watched the second. The room smelled of body odor and bad breath. I looked at the young men like they were a different type of human species. They wore sweatpants, polo shirts, and sandals. It felt like only seconds had passed when we heard another voice shout up the stairs, "Muhammad?!"

Still another Iraqi was walking up the stairs and we were running out of corners. Once again Decker and McGuire assumed their positions by the door. The third Iraqi stepped into the room and he too was tackled, muzzled, and zip-tied.

"Where is Bravo Two Six?" Howerton whispered with frustration.

"Hawk 3 Romeo, this is Bravo Two Six, we are here, over."

I snapped my head back to look at Mac who was kneeling behind me. He whispered, "They're here."

The Iraqis were left blindfolded, gagged, and zip-tied, kneeling in three different corners. We quickly made sure we had all our gear then quietly walked out of the room and down the stairs. We briefly gathered at the bottom of the stairs then left the building. We saw six Humvees from 2nd Platoon about fifty meters away, waiting for us on the road.

Meanwhile, the Iraqis stopped swinging their sledgehammers and were staring in awe at the soldiers who just pulled up. The Iraqis were unarmed, so we made a run for the Humvees. As we followed a trail through the rubble, the Iraqis stopped working, and while some stared at us, others fled. We loaded onto the trucks and made our way back to Baghdad International Airport (BIAP).

We confirmed there were no bombs left on that blown-out base, but we breathed some type of chemical that almost killed us. We debriefed the battalion commander, LTC Drinkwine, of our findings and we received a new mission.

Our battalion was going to convoy to a compound formerly belonging to Saddam's eldest son, Uday Hussein. Uday used the location as a resort for special guests. It featured a manmade lake, concrete huts, and palm trees, and it was nothing but nice. It was located in the center of the Sunni Triangle—or Triangle of Death—where the heaviest enemy resistance was taking place.

We would be conducting counter-insurgency operations in a city soon to become known as the most dangerous city in the world: Fallujah.

Chapter Thirteen

The Killer Inside

WHEN WE ARRIVED in Fallujah, we hit the ground running. We found ourselves being sporadically attacked by mortars and rockets around the clock.

After a few days of filling sandbags to reinforce our huts, and settling into our new living space, I went out on my first mission into the city. It was nighttime and before we left the forward operating base (FOB), we lined up in convoy formation by the front gate. I watched as hundreds of green tracer rounds soared from the city into the sky; I listened as the insurgents rallied in the streets with shouts of *Allahu akbar!*

Our Scout team was attached to the 10th Mountain Division Attack Company, and we were simply waiting for the clock to hit 2200 hours before leaving the wire and heading right for the insurgents. "Give us a few minutes—we'll be right there!" said the attack company commander, Captain Kirkpatrick, who added a few colorful insults.

I was sitting in the back of the Humvee while others were standing around their vehicles lined up in convoy formation. We were all looking toward the city and enjoying the fireworks show. Some troops were smoking cigarettes and making small talk. It was my first time going into Fallujah; all my buddies had already entered the city. And each time they entered, they engaged in a firefight with the enemy. I was still a "cherry" and the thought of going into the fire was unreal.

"Alright men, gather around!" shouted CPT Kirkpatrick. Chaplain Knight was going to lead us in a prayer before we headed into the darkness of Fallujah.

"Okay, men!" shouted Chaplain Knight as we gathered around him to form a circle. "Let us bow our heads in prayer. Dear Lord, we ask that You protect us from these animals we are about to face. We pray that You would keep us from any harm, but we ask that You guide our rounds, to hit the enemy in the face and send them to the depths of hell! We pray this in the name of Jesus, Amen."

With that, "Mount up!" shouted CPT Kirkpatrick and we got in our Humvees, fired up the engines, and drove outside the wire. We had ten Humvees with about eight soldiers per vehicle. Sitting to my left was SFC Lopez and to my right was CPL McGuire. The tracer rounds were still shooting across the sky as we drove toward the city, but when we hit a dirt road leading us into the east of Fallujah, the bullets stopped flying.

That meant we were being watched.

We drove using only IR (infrared) to light our path. We each wore PVS-14 night vision goggles, Surefire tactical flashlights with IR cap, PEQ-2 infrared lasers with flood lights, so we could see the city better than the enemy.

As we drove through the streets looking for a fight, I suddenly reported, "I've got a guy in the alley on his cell phone."

CPL McGuire grabbed the hand mic of his MIBTR and notified CPT Kirkpatrick. The captain responded with, "It's coming."

We knew the enemy was taunting us and we were here for a fight. We also knew the fight was likely going to be on their terms.

We drove around the city for about twenty minutes without any enemy contact, but tensions were high. We turned onto a road nicknamed "Ambush Alley" by the paratroopers, which ran along the Euphrates River on the outskirts of Fallujah looking for bad guys. Driving along Ambush Alley, I saw we were surrounded on both sides of the road by tall grass and swamp. Once our last vehicle followed, we were moving at about twenty miles per hour while continuing to scan the area. Suddenly CPL McGuire shouted to me. "Two-story house coming up; watch the windows!"

BOOM! BOOM! Two explosions were so close I felt the vibration in my chest. "RPGs!" shouted McGuire and Lopez. Two rockets flew past our Humvee just five feet over our heads.

"Ambush!" shouted McGuire as a flurry of green and red tracer rounds flew at us from behind the tall swamp grass. I felt a jolt as the driver of the Humvee floored the gas pedal to get us out of the kill zone. Without hesitation we returned fire. SFC Lopez had a two-hundred-round drum in his M-4 and McGuire lobbed 40mm grenades from his M-203 grenade launcher. I pointed my IR laser at insurgents moving and firing from the cover of the tall grass and fired on them.

"There's a guy running!" shouted McGuire. I aimed my PEQ-4 infrared laser on his chest and opened fire. I must have fired five rounds into the insurgent's chest and I watched as my tracer rounds entered and exited his body just before he was swallowed by the swamp.

"Changing mags!" I shouted and quickly dropped my magazine while reaching for another and reloaded my rifle. As I brought my rifle back up to shoot again, SFC Lopez yelled, "Cease fire, cease fire!" I quickly placed my weapon on safe. I felt multiple hands on my body. It was SFC Lopez and McGuire patting me down checking for blood. "Are you good?" McGuire asked me as he scanned my body.

"Yeah, I'm good."

Over the radio CPT Kirkpatrick's voice said we were turning our trucks around, and we were going to dismount and look for another fight. After we arrived back at the ambush sight, no one was there. There were traces of blood from the guys we shot, but no bodies. The enemy carried out their wounded. We mounted up and drove to our rest overnight (RON) site. There was a Bradley fighting vehicle already in position off Highway One, about a mile into the desert. We formed a circle, like wagons in the Old West, and started thirty-minute guard shifts. Everyone slept on cots or on the hood of the Humvees while soldiers manned the machine guns.

Once we settled in, I laid on my cot and reviewed the nights events. Like a video on a loop, I could see the rockets flying over me and I could hear the sonic boom the enemy's bullets made as they flew past me. I could see the man in black "man dress" running into the swamp as I pointed my IR laser at him and fired. I also fired into the windows of the two-story house and shot at a muzzle flash from behind the tall grass.

I didn't feel remorse for any of my actions and I didn't regret anything I did. The only thing bothering me, the only thing keeping me awake, and the only thing that scared me, was how quickly I fired back. That night wasn't my first time around guns and gun fire, but it was the first time I ever fired back. I was being praised by SFC Lopez and CPL McGuire for taking a life and fighting the enemy. In the airborne infantry, killing was a good thing, and that night I did a good job.

Chapter Fourteen

The Triangle of Death

I WAS IN Iraq for two months and already experienced several fire-fights, and mortar and rocket attacks. On October 20, 2003, while on a mission to provide security at the Fallujah mayor's office, A Company was hit by an ambush initiated by an IED rigged with a 105mm artillery round and two propane tanks. When the IED exploded, several paratroopers were wounded, and one of them, SSG Paul J. Johnson, was killed when shrapnel pierced his body armor and he caught fire from the propane flames. The paratroopers returned fire, killing several enemy combatants. SSG Johnson's death hit us hard. The truth is, as scary as combat was in Fallujah, it was fun. My buddies and I enjoyed every gun fight. We relished taking fire and returning fire. But as the saying goes, "It's fun until someone gets hurt."

The death of SSG Johnson reminded me of my humanness. I was a nineteen-year-old kid in combat gear, and I had the ability to make hellfire rain down from the sky on the enemy with just a call on the radio. But I was vulnerable too.

SSG Johnson was an experienced war fighter, having served in Afghanistan prior to our deployment to Fallujah. He was a battle-hardened, twenty-nine-year-old bad ass. We paid our respects to him, but we didn't have time to mourn. That is how it is in combat. You must keep fighting. You must keep moving forward. The only thing we could do to honor SSG Johnson was to kill as many enemy fighters as we were able. We were going to avenge him and make it known the 82nd

Airborne Division was the emissary of death. So, we got our kills. But the enemy always gets a vote.

As time went on during my deployment, I was exposed to the death, the destruction, and the mayhem of war, from which nobody is immune. The enemy would often engage us from crowds of pedestrians on just about any crowded street, in hopes we would not shoot for fear of killing innocent people, but that strategy didn't work. We did our best to engage accurately but sometimes the wrong people were hit. Men, women, and children suffered from those violent engagements. It was sickening, but my life and my buddies' lives were on the line.

If they hadn't shot at us, they would still be alive, I told myself.

One morning a group of insurgents stormed the Iraqi police station in Fallujah and a gun battle ensued. We heard the gunfire from our FOB. We put our gear on, mounted Humvees, and headed for the city. Our mission was to fight off the insurgents, but we were too late. By the time we got there, they were all dead. I'm not sure how many Iraqi policemen were killed, but we were ordered to bring some of their bodies back to base, as evidence of the incident.

I could hear the voice of the Charlie Company commander in the background, arguing with the battalion headquarters because he couldn't understand why it was necessary to bring "a few of the bodies back." While he argued over the radio, I was taking a knee behind a Humvee watching windows and rooftops in case the insurgents returned. I could hear AK-47s being fired in the distance by insurgents to signal our arrival. The Iraqi police station was a mess! I saw the bodies of about twenty or more dead policemen inside and scattered outside. The walls of the police station were splattered with blood and the insurgents made sure to scatter bodies on the streets as a display for us to see.

I felt bad for the privates of Charlie Company as a few of them were ordered to grab a few body bags and get at least two bodies to bring back to the FOB. I guess the company commander lost the argument and was following orders. Once the bodies were loaded on the trucks, we mounted our Humvees and returned to base. This attack on the Iraqi police station was one of the bloodiest days in Fallujah.

The stress of combat will make the toughest men seek psychological comfort. Death is an everyday reality, but no one would function if all they thought about was death and dying. At first, I prayed to God to keep me safe. I tried to remind myself God was with me, God was in control and heaven is real.

But as time went on in Fallujah, I started seeking comfort by thinking about Sarah. I hadn't set foot into a church service in several months, maybe even since airborne school. Instead, I thought about Sarah. I thought about holding her and feeling her soft skin with my hands as we kissed. Sarah and I wrote letters back and forth. She told me about her college experience, but I kept my experience vague. I called her on the phone about once a week when I had the chance. She told me she missed me and how great it was going to be when we were together again.

I knew we were falling in love, but I had to focus on the mission ahead.

Chapter Fifteen

Nighthawks

OUR MISSION WAS to rendezvous with the Army Special Missions Unit (SMU), British Special Air Services (SAS), and a platoon from the 75th Ranger Regiment (The Regiment) in the outskirts of Fallujah. Then we would head into the city and hit multiple homes where members of al-Qaeda in Iraq were staying. The targets of the SMU and The Regiment were classified. I knew what homes the SMU, SAS, and The Regiment were hitting, but without any details. And I knew the targets we would be hitting, in detail.

My team and I would secure a street corner to make sure no enemies entered or exited the target area. The Special Missions Unit and SAS drove into the city in Pandur-1 armored personnel carriers—APCs. These armored vehicles had six wheels, a turret for a machine gunner, and a square bulletproof window for the driver.

Once we were set, I watched a member of the SMU set explosives on the door of one of the target homes. He then pushed a button on his body armor as he signaled a countdown with his right hand, "3-2-1." I hadn't noticed the SAS and The Regiment had also set explosives on their target buildings as well. When the countdown ended, three explosions went off, almost simultaneously. At this point, I wasn't pulling security anymore, I was just watching the world's greatest warfighters carry out a mission to kill or capture a high value target (HVT). We hunted down HVTs in "The Deuce," also known as "The Division" (82nd Airborne). But I knew these HVTs were even higher up al-Qaeda's pecking order.

The three explosions were followed by a couple more as our invaders used flash-bang grenades to stun the enemy while they cleared the targeted homes. Several shots were fired as they swept through each house, killing anyone who posed a threat. Within seconds, the three homes were cleared and the call, "Beginning SSE" (sensitive sight exploitation) came over the radio. Our guys from B Co. also breached and cleared three homes and were carrying out SSE as well. Every laptop, cell phone, passport, weapon, and hard drive were collected for military intelligence personnel to examine.

That night we captured one of al-Qaeda leader Abu Musab Zarqawi's wives. That would come back to hurt us later on.

While I was on the street corner on a mission with the SMU, Scout Team 1 was busy in another part of Iraq, farther out from Fallujah. Egg and Sullivan later told me how the SMU knew our teams were conducting recon and sniper missions in a certain area outside Fallujah, so they asked Team 1 for help. SPC Egg, CPL McGuire, SSG Martin, SPC Sullivan, PFC Machado, and I met with a team from the SMU.

A command sergeant major (CSM) named John and his team were dressed in DCUs (desert camouflage uniform), hiking shoes, and tactical vests with Velcro communications gear with headphones and other gadgets none of us had ever seen before. Egg briefed John on the area of operations (AO) and told him about the roads, hot spots, and suspected AQI homes. The SMU CSM smiled, glad for the information and shared the battle plan.

Hawk 1 would serve as the sniper overwatch while the SMU and a platoon from Attack Company, 10th Mountain Division hit two houses. The target home of the SMU had a garage a few meters away suspected of housing a vehicle borne improvised explosive device (VBIED) car bomb. The house next door was suspected of having several AQI (al-Qaeda in Iraq) fighters serving as additional security for the VBIED.

The plan was for the SMU to drive toward the home with the VBIED, followed by the 10th Mountain, who would split off at a certain point to hit the house next door. As the SMU got close to their target house, they would call on the Spectre gunship hovering overhead to shoot the garage with its 105mm Howitzer, destroying the VBIED while simultaneously breaching and clearing their target home. The 10th Mountain was supposed to split and clear the second home, and Hawk 1 would stand off at a distance to provide sniper fire.

As the convoy of about ten vehicles approached the target buildings, the SMU called on the Spectre gunship to engage the garage. Through night vision goggles the powerful IR light of the specially equipped C-130 illuminated the garage to confirm the target. In a matter of seconds, the 105mm round streaked from the sky, destroying the garage and everything in it. Like a coordinated dance, the operators pulled up to their target home, exited the back of the Pandur, and breached the front door. A few flash-bang explosions and a few shots later, the house was clear.

Meanwhile, the 10th Mountain breached their target home, but the enemy was alerted by the garage-leveling explosion. An insurgent armed with a machine gun was waiting to greet the infantry platoon at the front door. As the first grunt entered the home, he was met with a volley of machine gun fire. The second and third man entering the home were also hit. One of the team leaders in the squad decided to throw a hand grenade into the first room to kill the machine gunner. As he threw the grenade in the room, he was shot in the hand holding the grenade. The grenade fell at the doorway and his entire squad was peppered with shrapnel from the hand grenade. Team 1, SSG Martin, Sullivan (Sully), Egg, Machado, and SPC Zavala left their sniper position to help with casualty evacuation.

The operators heard the gunfight and headed over to help. Team 1 carried out the wounded and provided first aid while 10th Mountain laid down suppressive fire.

"What the f--- is going on?!" yelled one of the operators.

"We're taking machine gun fire from the house! They knew we were coming!" yelled a 10th Mountain grunt.

"Get back! Get everyone out of here! We're gonna blow this s--- up!"

The call came over the radio for everyone to load up on the Humvees and drive away. When everyone was at a safe distance, the call came over the radio for the Spectre to "level the house." The warplane lit up the target building, then steel rain came down, destroying everything. An eerie silence followed the barrage from the gunship. The wounded were medically evacuated, and the mission was over.

Meanwhile, miles away, supply convoys were being targeted by insurgents in hopes of stopping necessary supplies from reaching our military bases. The commanders didn't pay much attention to this threat, until one day when several bases in the area reported having a water and food shortage. You can launch rockets and mortars into bases, you can shoot and harass supply convoys, but you never mess with our chow.

The brigade commander ordered our platoon to move to an old weapons factory and carry out missions to kill or capture those chow terrorists. Our Scout teams were separated for a few weeks, working with different units and carrying out different missions. Now we were going to reunite at the weapons factory and hunt the enemy together.

I couldn't wait.

Chapter Sixteen

The Brotherhood

WE WERE TOGETHER once again and it was good to see my brothers from the 1-505 Scouts. All of us "Joes" (lower enlisted) shared a special bond. We trained together, were hazed together, and endured the hardship of earning our keep in the Scout platoon. The saying went, "If you ain't tabbed, hit the slab!" My buddies and I didn't have our Ranger Tabs yet, so we were treated as less-than. It was due to our mutual misery we became close back at Bragg. We hugged each other as we reunited in front of a disgusting office-type building at the weapons factory.

Before we could unload the Humvees, we had to clean out the building. It was infested with rats (huge Iraqi rats that could kill a cat), camel spiders, and scorpions. We cleaned the building out and realized we needed furniture. SFC Lopez loved comfort and he had an epiphany. There was a very nice-looking office building, just a few miles down the highway from the weapons factory. The building stood out because it was a modern-looking five-story structure clad in glass, as if it were transported from the Avenue of the Stars in Century City, Los Angeles.

We drove to the building as a platoon, but we were briefed by an interpreter who was standing at the entrance with an Iraqi policeman. He told us we could take furniture but nothing else. We looked at each other bewildered because we were American paratroopers who were armed and dangerous. So we smiled at the request and entered. The interior of the building was awesome. It once belonged to the Iraqi army and was likely used as a department of defense headquarters, because it looked "official." Rosetta and I used the elevator to make our way to the fifth floor. When the doors opened, we were in a meeting room with tan-colored carpet, a beautiful oval-shaped mahogany table with black leather business chairs around it. At the opposite end from the elevator, hanging on the back wall, were two framed posters of Saddam Hussein.

Rosetta and I looked at each other, smiled, and each of us took one of the posters. We broke the frames, rolled up the posters, and put them in our cargo pockets. As we walked out of the building, the Iraqi police-men saw our posters and gave us angry looks. They instructed us not to take anything other than furniture, but we didn't care.

We took sofas, recliner chairs, tables, and a television from the office building to our new pad. We slept on green army cots, but our day room was something to envy, given the circumstances. We set up a TV room and we acquired "bootleg" DVD movies. We would use the TV room for hanging out and planning our missions. We happily settled into our new home.

"Tomorrow at 0900 hours, be in the TV room for the mission brief-ing," said Lt. Swartwood.

I stepped outside and gazed upon the nighttime sky. I could see every constellation and every shooting star in our galaxy. I thought about God and how He made everything. My countenance fell; I was suddenly overwhelmed with guilt. At this point in my deployment, I shot human beings, I captured and zip-tied some of them like animals. I called for mortar and attack helicopter fire on enemy fighters, and sur-vived several IED explosions. But I increasingly neglected God.

I whispered a prayer. "Lord, forgive me for my sins. I believe in You, but I must do bad things to bad people. I believe in You, but I have blood on my hands. Forgive me, Lord, for the evil I have done. Forgive me for looking for comfort in Sarah and not in You. But where are You? I'm out here fighting the enemy and You let SSG Paul Johnson die. And I'll do whatever I need to do to survive!"

Instead of feeling reverent and worshipful, I realized I was angry. And the truth was, right then, at that moment, thinking about Sarah offered me more comfort and peace in my heart than thinking about God.

Chapter Seventeen

The Hunting Party

WE RECEIVED THE mission brief at 0900 and it was scary. The insurgent force that terrorized the supply convoys was believed to be part of a sophisticated network of insurgents with ties to Abu Musab al-Zarqawi. It turned out we were living in a weapons factory previously providing employment to a few hundred Iraqi army personnel, who were now unemployed, and they hated America. The AQI supported and armed these Baath Party and Fedayeen—Saddam loyalists—to wreak havoc on American supply lines.

The Iranian government supplied weapons, explosives, and training to the insurgent forces. They were reported to stand their ground and even rush forward on the supply convoys. Lt. Swartwood and SFC Lopez warned us we needed to be ready to fight, hold our ground, and even push forward ourselves, which was not common in a recon unit.

"What support do we have, sir?" asked Mac.

"We have a platoon of QRF from Delta Company, an Anti-Tank (AT) section, armed with MK-19 40mm automatic grenade launchers, M-2 .50-caliber machine guns, TOW anti-tank missiles, 81mm mortars from the HQ mortar section, and OH-58 Kiowa helicopters from the 82nd Airborne Aviation Brigade, armed with 2.75-inch rockets and .50-caliber machine guns," Lt. Swartwood said, with a cocky smile on his face.

Hours passed and the sun set since the intelligence brief. I donned my body armor, helmet, knee pads, suppressed M-4, and ASIP radio. I mounted my PVS-14 night vision on my helmet, then PFC Knouse and

I walked toward the front perimeter gate of the weapons factory. It is unheard of for two soldiers, especially of the rank of private first class, to lock and load in a combat zone, and simply walk outside the base. We were recon, so we were in a privileged position of having a greater burden of responsibility than most soldiers.

As we walked to the front gate, manned by B Co. 1st Platoon, we locked and loaded our weapons, called the FOB sergeant of the guard (SOG), and informed him we were leaving the wire. As he acknowledged, I waved bye to my buddy SPC Weise who was manning a guard tower with his M-240B machine gun.

Earlier that week, Weise shot a suspected VBIED driver at a checkpoint, unloading 200 rounds of 7.62mm from his machine gun, into the man's upper body. After all that, Weise said, "I'm done," with a smile on his face. Weise was my bro, and I was happy to know he was watching my six.

Knouse and I left the wire on foot and walked to our overwatch position, about 3,000 meters from the front gate. When we reached our OP, I made the call to our PL.

"Hawk 6, this is Hawk 3 Romeo, we are putting [in position and conducting recon]."

"Hawk 3 Romeo, this is Hawk 6, that's a good copy, over."

"Hawk 3, out."

Knouse and I watched the road for about three hours, logging no activity. We whispered the whole time, sharing stories from our past, talking about our future when we returned to the states, thinking about our families back home, and Jesus Christ.

Knouse was a believer and we had conversations about our faith and the struggle of having to get "blood on our hands" while claiming to be Christians. As we whispered for several hours, I saw the headlights of a vehicle driving in our direction. From our position we could see several miles of Route San Jose, running from TQ (Al Taqaddum Airbase) and past the weapons factory. The vehicle slowed to a stop about 50 meters from our OP.

"Hawk 6 Romeo, this is Hawk 3 Romeo, over," I whispered into the hand mic.

"Hawk 3 Romeo, this is Hawk 6, over."

"I have a white Toyota Camry stopped about 50 meters from our OP. There is one occupant, and he is wearing a white man dress and a black-and-white checkered *shemagh*. Standby for further information, over."

Knouse and I watched the driver turn on his four-way flasher lights and exit the vehicle. He popped his hood open but didn't bother to look at his engine. He scanned the desert, looking for signs of any activity. Then he walked to the trunk of his car, opened it, and pulled out a shovel. He scanned the desert once more, but he couldn't see the two infrared lasers Knouse and I were pointing at his chest. Knouse had a suppressed M-4 and a clear shot. The rules of engagement stated we could fire on any fighting-age male who was digging a hole on the side of the road past curfew. Curfew was 2100, and it was 2300.

"Hawk 6, this is Hawk 3 Romeo, over."

"Hawk 3 Romeo, this is Hawk 6, over."

"The driver is a fighting-age male, and he is digging a hole on the side of the road, most likely to place an IED, over."

The insurgents worked in teams of three, where one man dug the hole, the second placed the bomb in the hole, and the third connected the remote detonator.

"Hawk 3 Romeo, this is Hawk 6. You are clear to engage, over."

I leaned over to Knouse and whispered, "Send it."

I heard the metallic *click* as he switched from "safe" to "semi" and fired into the man's chest. The insurgent dropped the shovel and ran to the driver seat. He shifted the car into drive and sped off. The next day we heard of a guy who was found dead in his car, several miles from our OP.

This same scenario played out for several nights, but the truth was most nights were uneventful and boring. When winter came around, it was freezing. Knouse and I spooned, using a military issued poncho liner (woobie) to cover our bodies and hold body heat. We were two dudes, spooning under a woobie, and whispering into each other's ears for eight hours a night. No Army commercial will ever show this type of stuff, but being in a recon/sniper team meant we did this a lot in the winter. I knew everything about Knouse and he knew everything about me. The best thing about those cold nights was when we shot someone. Either we shot their car or shot the driver, but engaging the enemy meant we had to return to base for fear our position was compromised and follow-on enemy forces could attack us. And that meant we could get warmed up.

On one cold and miserable night, around 0100 hours, Knouse and I were "snuggled up" under the woobie while watching the road. Just about 50 meters from our position, a guy driving a white sedan stopped his vehicle at our two o'clock. He exited the vehicle, opened the trunk of his car, and pulled out a shovel. "It's your turn to shoot," Knouse whispered in my ear. I aimed for the driver, but he disappeared on the opposite side of the car where he was digging. I waited a few minutes for him to reappear. The man was wearing a white robe, sandals, and a black leather jacket.

When he reappeared, he quickly walked to the trunk, opened it and tossed the shovel in, then slammed it shut. Then he quickly got into the driver's seat and put the car in drive, but he didn't move. I could see him put his cell phone to his ear, probably letting the next guy know the hole was ready for a bomb to be inserted.

That pause gave me the time I needed for a clear shot. I took aim, pointing my IR laser through his rear window, targeting the back of the driver seat. I could feel my heart beating in the temples of my head, like I was running in high altitude and my brain was starving for oxygen. I pushed downward with my thumb, placing my weapon from safe to semi. I slowly squeezed the trigger and felt the recoil of the buttstock on my shoulder as I fired one well-placed round that penetrated the rear windshield, through the driver seat, and through the man's rear torso.

When the bullet impacted his back, I watched the driver slump over the steering wheel. He quickly leaned back on his seat, turned on his four-way lights, and drove off slowly, at about twenty miles per hour. When his lights disappeared at a distance, Knouse and I were happy we were going back to the weapons factory to warm cots and a hot meal.

A few days later, I was at the weapons factory, enjoying some quality time with the boys, when I heard soldiers shouting, "We got him! We got him!" Our platoon went outside to see what was going on. It was December 13, 2003, and the SMU had carried out an operation dubbed Operation Red Dawn. It ended with the capture of Saddam Hussein. We talked among ourselves wondering how this would affect us. We all agreed nothing was going to change, so we went right back to relaxing before the next night of hunting.

We lived in the weapons factory for several weeks, searching for insurgents at night and hitting them with 81mm mortar fire when we had the chance. The IEDs and ambushes dropped drastically and the supply convoys were able to make their deliveries with minimal harassment. Now that our base had plenty of water and chow, we were called to return to FOB Volturno in Fallujah. It would be our job to deal with the mortar attack problem, and with the insurgents in and around the city.

Chapter Eighteen

Home Invasion

"INCOMING!" I YELLED to the platoon as mortar rounds exploded ever closer to our hut. This was an almost nightly occurrence happening between the hours of 2100 to 2300. We would lie in our bunks, some sleeping while others stayed awake, and wait for the rounds to be fired. It was like the scene from the movie *Jurassic Park*, where a distant "thud" was heard and everyone wondered what it was as the thud grew louder and louder, until the T-Rex appeared.

A distant thud could be easily mistaken as a boot or a helmet lightly hitting a concrete wall in our hut, but after several months of being in Fallujah, I knew better.

"Incoming!"

Everyone echoed the words, as we donned our combat gear. I leaned against a wall next to PFC Hunt and Sully and we looked at each other in annoyance, waiting for the rounds to impact, so we could go to sleep.

Boom! One after another the mortars detonated upon contact with the earth around our hut or on the rooftop. Thank God those buildings were made of concrete. The rounds exploded, and then the night was quiet again, so we took off our gear and went back to sleep. We dubbed our nightly team of attackers the "Mad Mortarmen." For several months we went out on missions to kill this team of terrorists, but we kept getting called to do other missions and never gave them the justice they deserved.

A few nights before, the Mad Mortarmen were successful in killing an interpreter on our FOB. The interpreter was a part of the intel team,

Prowler 13, and was sitting in a porta john, when the Mad Mortarmen fired several times, and one mortar exploded a few feet next to the porta john, sending shrapnel through the interpreter's body.

But this night was different. We slept four hours and then got ready for a home invasion. The commander of forces in Iraq, General Abizaid, and the commander of the 82nd Airborne Division, General Swannack, escorted by the entire 1-505 PIR, were scheduled to visit the new mayor's office to meet with city leaders and discuss important "stuff."

Our mission was to prevent the Mad Mortarmen from launching rounds into the city, and possibly to kill the Mad Mortarmen team. I couldn't sleep because of the anticipation of what might lie ahead, so I lay in my bed pretending to sleep. I thought about Sarah all night, smelling the envelope of the last letter she sent me, which she sprayed with her perfume.

Before I knew it, it was time to get ready. We got on our feet, grabbed our gear, and loaded up on the Humvees. We met at Gate 1 with a squad from A Co. and headed out. The home we were commandeering was in the outskirts of Fallujah, so the city lights didn't affect my view of the stars in the sky through my PVS-14s. I was on my way to carry out a home invasion with a crew of killers but, looking up at the stars, I thought about God. And I offered up another silent prayer: *Lord, forgive me for my sins. Keep us safe tonight and, if I die, take me with You. Amen.*

We pulled up to the two-story home and quickly dismounted our Humvees. We stacked on the front door, behind the squad from A Co., as they breached the door and cleared the home. "All call signs, house is clear," I heard over the radio. I walked into the living room behind our new lieutenant, Lt. O'Brian, and saw a family of a husband, a wife, and four children, sitting in the corner of the living room, looking startled. Lt. O'Brian and I approached the man of the house as the rest of Team 3 headed for the rooftop to establish sniper and OP positions.

"What is happening?" asked the man of the house through an interpreter.

"We need to stay in your home for twenty-four hours," said Lt. O'Brian. "We're sorry to scare you, but we will pay you to stay here."

Lt. O'Brian pulled out two hundred American dollars, and the man's eyes lit up. Suddenly, having his home invaded and his family terrified wasn't so bad. Lt. O'Brian handed the man the money and he warmly thanked O'Brian. We then made our way to the rooftop and joined the rest of Team 3. Mac had already given each Scout sniper a sector of fire and started a rest plan. Gibson and I were the first to sleep, while Mac, O'Brian, Knouse, and PFC Baylor conducted surveillance.

At the end of the stairway leading to the roof, was a pile of rebar. In the rebar was a rat nest. The house was also infested with rats. As usual, these Iraqi rats were huge. They were also fearless. I couldn't sleep for fear of one of them biting me. But next to me, Gibson was sleeping like a baby. I watched as the rats poked their heads out from the rebar, staring at me. There must have been fifty of them in there.

I heard a squeak to my right, and I looked down to see two rats smelling PFC Gibson's face while he was sleeping. I waved my arm, and they ran away, but not far. They only moved back about three feet before they turned around and started to slowly make their way back to Gibson's face. I sat with my legs crossed feeling creeped out. I looked around me and four rats were at my boots, sniffing away. After about an hour of being disgusted by these filthy creatures, I just didn't care anymore. They sniffed my boots and my pant legs and came close enough for me to pet them, but they didn't bother me.

"Sun's out, guns out," Mac told me. The call came over the radio, "All American 6"—the call sign for the visiting generals—was en route to Fallujah. I was staring through the M3 Alpha (M3A) scope mounted on the Barrett .50-caliber sniper rifle, looking for enemy activity. Everything was quiet for the couple of hours the two generals were in the city. Then the call came over the radio, "All American 6 is moving out." The two commanders were in their respective Humvees and driving back to FOB Volturno. They were about a mile away by a gas station, on ramps by Highway 1 near the Cloverfield, an interchange on the highway entering the city of Fallujah. Suddenly, bullets started flying.

Two RPGs were fired from the gas station and missed General Abizaid's Humvee. B Co. 1st Platoon and Team 2 returned fire, killing the gunmen. Across the street from the gas station several gunmen appeared wearing ski masks, and AK-47 tactical chest rigs. The Humvees with Generals Abizaid and Swannack kept moving as a Bradley fighting vehicle opened fire with its 25mm Bushmaster chain cannon, turning Zarqawi's men into pink mist. The Bradley's .50-caliber gunner opened fire on the driver of a vehicle loaded with AQI. The vehicle was stopped in the street and blood covered the interior of the windows.

"Hey, Doc!" shouted an NCO from C Co.

"What, Sergeant!"

"Go check and see if anyone is alive!" The call was referring to the car with the bloody windows.

Doc Joe "the Mouth" Connell (because he liked to insult people) walked toward the vehicle and opened the driver door. The driver's forehead rested on his own right shoulder, after the .50-caliber round pierced his neck. The other occupants looked like ground beef. They were unidentifiable.

"They're all dead!" shouted Doc the Mouth.

"Alright, load up!"

Hunt and PFC Garza were tasked with picking up and placing into body bags the two RPG shooters from the gas station. They tried to open a body bag and then pick up and place the first shooter in it, but it was more difficult than it looked. The body bag didn't seem wide enough, and the insurgent's brains were oozing out his skull, making a mess. Hunt asked for help and some guys from B Co. held the body bag open so Garza and Hunt could place the body inside. The next one wasn't so hard to put in the bag once they figured out the proper method of insertion.

Hours after the fighting was over and the sun was set, the kind people—whose home we invaded—thanked us for our stay and said goodbye. I shook hands with the men, but we were never to touch the women.

I spoke to Hunt when I got back to the FOB. He had adopted the thousand-yard stare, and his skin was pale as a white crayon. That night he looked like he'd seen a ghost. He described to me what it was like to carry a dead guy while his brains were oozing from his skull. I thought he was going to vomit as he paused a few times when he described the yellowish color of brain fluid. I wasn't a smoker, but that night I smoked a couple of cigarettes with him until he felt better. I hugged him and told him I loved him. I saw the bodies of the Iraqis he was talking about. They were at the battalion headquarters in open body bags and I saw that same brain matter oozing out of their skulls.

At the young age of nineteen I learned that in combat you have to put your emotions aside, because the next mission is just around the corner.

Chapter Nineteen

The Mad Mortarmen

OPERATION MAD MORTARMEN was a go. It wasn't really called that, but we joked around as we were preparing our gear for the mission. We were finally given orders to hunt these guys down because of a situation created by the Army SMU.

Earlier that week, when I was on the mission with the SMU and SAS, the SMU captured some of Zarqawi's lieutenants, and one of his wives. The city of Fallujah was in an uproar because it is considered a huge disrespect to touch Arab women. Zarqawi ordered the continual bombing of our FOB until we released his wife. For twenty-four hours our base received about one mortar and rocket attack per hour. The Iranians helped AQI develop makeshift rocket launchers that could be fired from over thirty miles away. They were launching these rockets throughout the day and into the night.

That afternoon I was in the morale, welfare, and recreation (MWR) hut on our FOB. There were phones and computers available to us, which was a huge morale boost. I was on the phone with my mom when rockets rained down on our FOB.

"*Mijo*, what is that noise?" my mom asked with concern.

"It's nothing, Mom. Just some construction going on to install new phones."

"Really? It sounds loud, *mijo*. Are you okay?"

"Yeah, Mom. I'm alright. Look, it's getting loud, and I have to go because I can't hear you, okay?"

"Okay. I love you, *mijo*."

"Bye, Mom."

I was pissed! These dudes were ruining my entire day with their bombs. About thirty minutes later, when the rocket attack was over, I called Sarah. We were talking about our future together and joking about how our kids would look and behave. I told her they would have her eyes and my sense of humor. Talking to Sarah helped me escape Iraq and made me feel like I wasn't in combat anymore. For those few minutes I was able to talk to her, I was with her. It was like my fuel tank was empty and talking to her filled me up and energized me.

But then there was another *Boom!* And now Sarah was worried.

"Fernando, what's going on?!"

"It's just some construction. They're trying to install new phones. I'm sorry the hammers are so loud."

"I know you're lying to me! There's something wrong. Tell me, what is it?"

"I have to go. Sorry, Sarah, but I have to go."

I hung up the phone. When the attack was over, I headed to dinner chow. After dinner I met up with Mac, McGuire, Lopez, Baylor, Knouse, and PFC Gibson at the gym when incoming mortars started raining down on our FOB. It was around 1700 hours.

"It's gotta be the Mad Mortarmen!" McGuire shouted, as paratroopers and SMU operators in the gym tried to find cover.

"Listen!" shouted SFC Lopez. "That sounds like 50 cals!" SFC Lopez served as a Recon Marine and eventually joined the Army, earned his Ranger Tab, and served as a combative instructor in the Ranger School. This was his fourth combat deployment, and he knew a .50-caliber when he heard one.

We stopped our workout, hopped on the Humvees, and hauled ass back to the hut. I could hear the Barretts going off louder as we got closer. When we got close to our huts the shooting was over. When we got there, Sully, Egg, Hunt, Garza, Machado, and Rosetta were all laughing and high-fiving each other. When the mortars started landing in our FOB, Egg and Hunt happened to be on the roof of one of the huts and could see the flash from the 82mm mortar tubes as they fired into our FOB. They called on the other guys to bring the .50-cal. rifles up to the roof, so the Scouts scrambled to gather the rifles, spotting scopes, and thermal scopes.

Using their DOPE (data of previous engagement) sniper books, they adjusted their scopes and engaged two vehicles at almost a mile away, as the sun was setting. They observed two vehicles—a white van and a white pickup truck in which the insurgents would transport the second mortar tube and extra ammo. Egg said he saw six men with two mortar tubes, so he began to fire. They shot two of them using .50-caliber, armor piercing incendiary (API) rounds. After that engagement, the Mad Mortarmen didn't shoot into our FOB for a week. But they eventually returned, and with a vengeance. The Mad Mortarmen were firing two to three times a night. That's what it took for them to get the attention of Lieutenant Colonel Drinkwine, our battalion commander, and our Command Sergeant Major, Bryant "Debo" Lambert.

"Hey Muldoons, kill 'em—kill 'em all." CSM Lambert gave us the orders and Operation Mad Mortarmen was a go.

Lt. O'Brian gave us on Team 3 the mission. O'Brian and Mac gave the operations order together, allowing Mac to give the situation, mission and execution portion, while O'Brian gave the service and support, and command and signal portions. I was pumped up and ready. These Mad Mortarmen terrorized us for six months, and now we were going to hunt them down.

The entire Scout platoon was on this mission. The other two Scout teams were going to serve as a QRF nearby while Team 3 split into two, three-man teams on both sides of Highway 10. Knouse, CPL Taylor, and I were on one side, and Mac, Baylor, and Gibson were on the other. We were also about a half mile away from each other so we could cover more ground and not shoot at each other.

Every hour we made radio checks, letting everyone know we were alive. A couple of hours passed, and it was 2100 hours or "Mortar O'clock" as we called it. Nothing was happening. 2200 hours came and went, and nothing was happening; 2300 hours and our morale was low. I felt disappointed and, when 0000 hours came along, I thought it was over. The mission was a failure, and we would have to come back out another night to finally get the Mad Mortarmen.

It was 0100, when Knouse, Taylor, and I were just talking, not whispering since we could see around us for miles, sharing funny stories from back home.

"Hawk 3 Romeo, this is 1 Panther 71, over."

"1 Panther 71, this is Hawk 3 Romeo, over."

"Hawk 3 Romeo, this is 1 Panther 71, we have intercepted radio chatter that a mortar attack on our FOB is underway, over."

I told my team what I just heard, and we looked around us. There was nothing. No vehicles on the road, no movement, there was no suspicious activity. We were all wearing night vision, Knouse had the thermal scope, and we scanned the landscape. There was nothing.

"1 Panther 71, this is Hawk 3 Romeo, over," I whispered over the hand mic, because we were back on "tactical mode."

"Hawk 3 Romeo, this is 1 Panther 71, go ahead, over."

"1 Panther 71, we do not see any enemy—"

Before I could finish, I saw three flashes of light, and heard three booms from the mortars being fired. It was the Mad Mortarmen. They were 200 meters away in the small white pickup truck and the white van. I went to work and called in a fire mission.

"Blaster 5, this is Hawk 3 Romeo, adjust fire polar, over."

"Hawk 3 Romeo, this is Blaster 5, adjust fire polar, out."

"Blaster 5, this is Hawk 3 Romeo, my grid is LB [Lima Bravo was the Fallujah map]—over."

"LB—out."

"Direction, 2400 mils, over."

"Direction, 2400 mils, out."

"Distance, 200 meters, over."

"Distance, 200 meters, out."

"Description, six troops in the open, in two white vehicles, over.

"Troops in the open, in two white vehicles, out."

As the seconds passed and I waited for the mortar crew to fire, I heard a voice on my radio.

"Break, break, break . . . This is Iron 13 [one three], over."

"Iron 13, this is Hawk 3 Romeo, over."

"Hawk 3 Romeo, confirm the enemy location. Over."

It was the 105mm Howitzer artillery section, the "big guns," and their radar triangulated the source of the Mad Mortarmen, but they wanted my confirmation to engage.

"Iron 13, that's a good copy. Ten rounds, fire for effect, over."

I could hear the 105mm Howitzers firing from over five miles away. It was louder than the 81mm mortars, who were probably angry because the 105s stole their show. I watched as 105mm Howitzer rounds ended the Mad Mortarmen. When the fire mission was complete, a Kiowa helicopter came on scene, and I directed the pilot to the mortar position, but they said there wasn't anything there.

In the morning, C Co. sent out a platoon to do a battle damage assessment. They found a white pickup truck with blood stains and shrapnel holes all around it. There were also two 82mm mortar tubes, 82mm mortar rounds, and a few AK 47s. The Mad Mortarmen carried out their dead, loading them into the van and drove off. I don't know how or why, but C Co. claimed credit for defeating the Mad Mortarmen because they were the ones who found the weapons they left behind.

Although I was annoyed by this, I kept my mouth shut. I knew what our team accomplished that night. I called in a strike package on the Mad Mortarmen and they got a taste of American steel rain. I hated the mortarmen and I wished I was able to watch them bleed while they screamed from the pain of their wounds. The Mad Mortarmen were defeated and the mortar attacks on our FOB stopped.

Chapter Twenty

Road Trip

MY DEPLOYMENT TO Iraq came to an end. The 1st Marine Expeditionary Force was set to relieve our battalion in Fallujah, and Knouse, Gibson, Baylor, and I were scheduled to drive the Scout Humvees from Fallujah to Kuwait. The truth is, I didn't want to leave. I wanted to go home to spend some time with Sarah, then return to Fallujah. I loved combat. The adrenaline of war was greater than any excitement I ever experienced.

As my buddies and I made our way to Kuwait, the men of B Co. 1st Platoon were on their last mission to provide security to the mayor's cell (headquarters).

About nineteen Marines and paratroopers were standing guard on the rooftop of the mayor's cell when a call came over the radio—the people in the city were reporting a mortar team was setting up to fire just outside the city. By the time this message was relayed to the paratroopers and Marines on the rooftop, it was too late.

Zarqawi and his goons were back for more. And this time, they wouldn't miss.

A mortar landed right in the middle of the rooftop, injuring every paratrooper and Marine. When the dust cleared, several paratroopers, despite their wounds, helped to evacuate the injured Marines. Weise and the men of 1st Platoon, and Scout teams 1, 2, and 3, opened fire on the enemy fighters in the city. Weise, PFC Kesler, PFC Viola, Rosetta, Baylor, Taylor, and everyone else on that rooftop were covered in shrapnel. Doc Llanas performed first aid on the Marines first, while the paratroopers fought. This was the final mission for the 82nd Airborne in Fallujah.

As the last troops of the 1-505 PIR left Fallujah, they were asked by Marine commanders for their names, ranks, and social security numbers. The Marine commanders told the paratroopers they would receive medals for their actions on the rooftop, to include the Navy Cross. That never happened. But as the last of the paratroopers left FOB Volturno, now Camp Fallujah, the Marines assembled an Honor Guard, lining each side of the road leading to Gate 1, with the American flag and Marine Corps colors. They saluted the paratroopers and gave them full honors as they left the FOB.

As for me, I was on an airplane to Fort Bragg, North Carolina, and I arrived at Pope Air Force Base. I remember exiting the airplane and seeing trees, a clean airport, and American troops. They were wearing woodland BDU camouflage, which somehow looked strange to me.

I carried the Barrett .50-cal. sniper rifle, my M-4 and everything else. I walked out of the hangar to the outer wall and sat. I looked around, scanning the vegetation and North Carolina scenery. It was surreal. I eventually returned to the barracks, turned in all the combat equipment I carried and relied on for self-defense and the defense of my buddies. I unlocked the door to my barracks. I had my own room.

That night, I awoke at around 0200 hours and I dove out of my bed because the Mad Mortarmen were attacking. I went to grab my body armor, helmet, weapon, and night vision from next to my bunk, but they weren't there. My heart was pounding in my chest as I heard the incoming rounds exploding all around me. "Hawk 3 Romeo, this is 1 Panther 71, we need you to engage the enemy, over." I heard the radio calls, but I was too busy frantically looking under my bed and my closet for my combat gear, but it wasn't anywhere to be found. I looked out my barracks window and saw another three-story barracks building and a green wood line in the background. That's when it hit me . . . I wasn't in Iraq anymore.

I took several deep breaths and, when I calmed down, I went back to bed.

Chapter Twenty-One

Shell Shock

BACK HOME IN Bell Gardens, I was enjoying my time with Sarah. It was great to see her, to feel her lips on my lips and to love her. I was certain she was the woman I would spend the rest of my life with. This time, Sarah noticed I was hypervigilant while driving. "Why do you keep looking down every street and alley, like you're a cop?"

I didn't answer. As far as I was concerned, I was just keeping us safe from any attack or IED.

One day I was watching TV in the living room with my mom, when I heard a loud *thud* from the back alley.

"Incoming! Get the f--- down!" I yelled as I dove onto the living room floor.

I was facedown in my parents' living room, looking for my M-4 and combat gear, but it wasn't there.

"*Mijo!* Are you okay!" my mom yelled at me.

Again, I remembered I was in my parents' home, in Bell Gardens and in a safe place. I got up from the floor laughing out loud at myself. I sat back down and continued watching TV like nothing happened.

"*Mijo*, are you sure you're okay?" my mom whispered again, concerned I might snap if she startled me.

"Yeah, Mom. I'm okay." I laughed as I said it because I felt silly.

I saw my mother's eyes get watery as she realized her baby was *not* okay.

"I'm okay, Mom," I laughingly said again, chuckling as a tear went down her cheek.

I repeated, "Really, Mom, I'm okay."

Chapter Twenty-Two

The Arena

IT WAS A warm morning at Fort Bragg, North Carolina, and I was back from my two-week vacation, after returning from Fallujah. I was there among 200 or more of the best paratroopers in the division. We were standing on the Towle Stadium field, waiting for the Ranger instructors (RI) to arrive. My time had come to earn my place as a Scout by earning my Ranger Tab. Without the Ranger Tab, no Scout could remain in the platoon or hold a leadership position. I was nervous because I heard all the Ranger School horror stories of guys sleepwalking, dumpster diving, and talking to trees after being deprived of food and sleep for several days.

Before I could attend Ranger School, I had to pass the Pre-Ranger Course (PRC) which was designed to weed out the guys who were not physically and mentally prepared, and to ready those who would go to Ranger School, to succeed.

The RIs arrived in two Humvees and a five-ton truck. They wore black T-shirts with a huge gold Ranger Tab and black silk shorts, affectionately called "Ranger panties." They set up their folding chairs about two-arms distance from each other and we evenly lined up in front of each station. The first event of the day was the physical fitness test. It consisted of two minutes of push-ups, two minutes of sit-ups, a two-mile run, six pull-ups, a twenty-five-meter swim in combat gear with a dummy M-16 rifle, a thirty-foot jump into the pool after being blindfolded and spun around, then removing all our gear before surfacing.

This was a competition. There were over 200 of us, but only fifty of us could advance to the next level.

I pushed myself in every event, determined to earn my position in the PRC and to begin my several months' journey to earn the Ranger Tab. I pushed, ran, pulled, and swam as best I could. When it was over, some had already quit, and others failed. We stood by the five-ton truck in BDUs, boots, patrol caps (PC), and duffel bags, waiting to hear the names of the fifty men who would load their bags on the truck and make the drive to PRC. About twenty names passed before I heard my name.

I loaded my duffel bags on the truck and hopped in. The drive to PRC was about thirty minutes. PRC was out in the woods in what used to be Recondo School during the Vietnam era. It was made up of a few trailers with bunk beds and classrooms. The back of the truck was covered in a green tarp, so we couldn't see where we were, which added to the anxiety of wanting to know how soon my three weeks of torture would begin.

The truck stopped and the back flap of the tarp was lifted. I saw we were stopped on a fire break in the woods. An RI said, "Alright, Rangers, dismount from the truck, grab all your gear, and walk that way." He pointed, using a knife hand motion, toward the direction of the road we were to follow.

The sun was up, and it was about 95 degrees with 100 percent humidity. I carried my rucksack on my back, with a duffel bag on top of it. My M-4 was slung around my chest, and my second green duffel bag was in my arms in front of me. We hadn't walked far when we made our way around a bend on the road, and I saw four RIs standing next to several 5-gallon water jugs, and a few tactical litters, with 160-pound dummies on them. An RI yelled, "Alright, Rangers! Your mission is to get all of this down the road to camp. Too easy, Rangers!"

Everyone grabbed something. I placed my second duffel bag on my rucksack, on top of my other one, and I grabbed two water jugs and I started walking toward the camp. About one minute into the walk, I heard the whistle from an arti-sim (artillery simulator). "Incoming!"

I dropped to the ground, then I heard the explosion. "Twelve o'clock, 300 meters!" We echoed the command, "Twelve o'clock, 300 meters!"

I struggled to get my duffel bags back on my rucksack, grabbed the two water jugs, and ran as fast as I could farther down the fire break.

"Incoming!"

I dropped again until the explosion. "Twelve o'clock, 300 meters!" I got back up and kept running with all my gear. This went on for about thirty minutes until we reached the PRC camp.

We were told to ground our gear in a field and we traveled up and down a hill, either running up and down, bear crawling up and running down, crab walking up and running down, or many other variations. After two hours of this, several students quit. The punishment continued, until I noticed another student looking pale and clammy as we ran up the hill for the hundredth time. I heard him mumbling to himself, so I asked him if he was okay. He collapsed, facedown in the dirt. Several of us picked him up and carried him uphill to one of the RIs. The RIs carried MIBTR radios, so one of them grabbed his hand mic and called in a 9-line medevac.

We carried the paratrooper to the field while another RI threw a smoke grenade as the sound of helicopter rotors grew louder. The UH-1 Huey appeared from above the tree line with a red cross symbol on each door. We took a knee around the student to protect him from the debris of the propellers, then we carried him to the helicopter.

"Back up!"

The helicopter crew chief yelled at us, after we loaded the Ranger student into the bird. We stayed low and cleared away from the helicopter, then turned around and watched it go up and forward, into the sky. This all happened in just a few minutes. We stared until the chopper disappeared in the distance. Then we turned toward the four RIs, who were staring with us. We were all combat proven paratroopers, and the medevac helicopter brought back somber memories of friends who were wounded or killed in action. The RIs looked at us.

"That's why we tell you to drink water! Now get your asses back to the hill!"

There was no mercy here. For the next three weeks we were pushed to our physical and mental limits. In between getting smoked and eating meals, we were taught everything there is to know about small unit tactics (SUT), ambush, raid, recon, and movement to contact missions. We learned everything from receiving and planning the mission, coordinating mortar and artillery fire, helicopter air assault operations, vehicle-mounted operations, and executing the mission. PRC was the community college for warfighters and Ranger School was the University. I was on my way to earning my bachelor's degree in warfare.

The third and final week of PRC, we were out in the woods, practicing everything we learned, while being graded on our leadership skills. We slept about an hour each night and were given one meal a day. It was my turn to be graded as a squad leader in charge of carrying out an ambush. I set up the L-shaped ambush on the curving part of a road where the intelligence brief said an enemy convoy of two vehicles filled with terrorists would drive through in fifteen minutes.

That meant I had fifteen minutes to set up a hasty ambush. I put my three machine gun teams on the curve of the road where they would be able to shoot the front and driver side of the vehicles. Then I set up my ambush line about ten meters off the road, giving everyone sectors of fire, making sure everyone's sectors were interlocking at twenty-five meters or hand grenade range.

My ambush line was set, with five minutes to spare. Everyone in the ambush line was camouflaged with face paint, and covered in vegetation so the enemy wouldn't see us. I heard vehicles approaching and I received a call on my radio, from the security team down the road, that the enemy was approaching. "Three cargo Humvees, carrying about eight enemy fighters total, just passed us." I waited for the middle vehicle to pass in front of the Claymore mine (a directional antipersonnel weapon containing approximately 1.5 pounds of C4 plastic explosive and embedded approximately 700 steel ball bearings) and then initiated the ambush. We used an artillery simulator as a Claymore, and we fired blank rounds. We unloaded hundreds of rounds into the enemy convoy.

"Cease fire, cease fire, cease fire!" I shouted to the ambush line and machine gun teams. We moved toward the vehicles and made sure all enemy combatants were dead. I had ten minutes before the enemy QRF would arrive, so I had to act fast. I had my squad search every combatant for intel, such as maps, electronic devices, etc., and then we disappeared into the woods. Once we were about fifty meters away from the site, I called in field artillery to drop ten rounds of 105mm high explosive (HE) rounds. The ambush was a success.

At the end of the three weeks of training, I was one of the remnant surviving PRC. It was graduation day, and we were back at division headquarters. Of the 200 men who arrived on the first day, only fifty of us were selected to attend PRC, and of the fifty men who made it to PRC, only fifteen of us graduated.

I was on my way to Ranger School.

Chapter Twenty-Three

Failure

I WAS STANDING among warriors. Men from the Infantry Basic Officer Leader Course (IBOLC), the 75th Ranger Regiment, Marine Recon, and Force Recon, Air Force Special Operations, Navy SEALs, and many others were all here. I stood in formation next to my two duffel bags, waiting for the physical fitness test to begin. It was 0500 and we lined up in front of several stations where RIs sat in their foldable chairs to grade us, just like PRC. I passed the physical fitness test and loaded on a bus headed for the swim test. I stood in line outside of the pool facility, waiting to be called in for the swim test, when I heard someone shout,

"Where is he?!"

Another RI said, "Who are you looking for?"

"He knows who he is."

I was standing at attention, looking straight ahead, when I saw the RI through my peripheral view. He was looking right at me.

"There you are," he said as he walked toward me from my right side. I turned to look at him, it was SSG Eton, from Airborne School. He was now an RI in the 4th Ranger Training Battalion.

"Are you ready for this?"

"Yes, Sergeant."

"You better be." With that, he walked away.

I passed the swim test and returned to our duffel bags. We were smoked for several hours until lunch time. Then we were smoked for several more hours until dinner time. Then we did combatives for even more hours, stopping only to get smoked again. We were pitted against each other, switching partners, wrestling opponent after opponent to the ground until 0200. At 0200 we were tasked with making a fire guard list, securing our duffel bags in a wall locker, and making a list of bunk assignments. It was all busy work to keep us from sleeping. When we finished these tasks, we slept for about an hour, and it was day two of potentially sixty-two days.

Day two started with a day/night land navigation test. We were given maps and our grid location. Then we were given a sheet with ten points to find. To pass the test, in five hours we had to find seven out of ten points. The distance between points varied from 1,000 meters to 2,500 meters. During the land nav brief, the RI said, "Trust your pace count, Rangers. There are dirt roads out there that are not on your map. Trust your pace count so that you don't go down the wrong road."

I headed out to find my first point. We were not allowed to talk to other students, and it was rumored that RIs, dressed in ghillie suits, were watching the students in case they decided to cheat. I walked through the woods, keeping my pace count, when I encountered a dirt road. According to my pace count, the road I was looking for was only fifteen meters away.

Is this it? I said to myself.

I looked ahead but it didn't appear there was another road. I realized I was lost. I had to backtrack to where I was before, re-plot my grid, get my azimuth (direction using the degrees in a compass), and start moving. I was falling behind on the clock. As the night progressed, I found six points, but I had twenty minutes left to find my seventh. Each point had a number I had to write on the paper I was given, and each point had a hole puncher with different patterns to make sure I was at the point. When I reached my seventh point, the hole puncher was missing. I looked in the bushes around the point, but I couldn't find it. I was running out of time, so I wrote down the number and ran back to the finish point. I handed my paper to an RI and he said, "Where is the hole punch on this point?" I explained to him there was no hole puncher on that point, but he didn't care. I failed.

~ ~ ~

I was recycled and would continue Ranger School in three weeks, when the next class started. As more soldiers failed and were recycled, I met guys from different units. One man I got to know well was Grant, with the 7th Special Forces Group, and he explained different things to me, like how to establish and manage human intelligence sources. Being a recycle in Ranger School was like being in jail where, as criminals learn new ways to commit crimes, I learned different tactics for entering and clearing rooms, breaching and hand-to-hand combat.

One day a new recycle student joined our group. He was thin and he slept most of the time. His name was Price, and he was with the 2nd Battalion, 75th Ranger Regiment Recon platoon. He looked spiritually broken, like he suffered some type of loss. I asked him why he was recycled, and he told me he was in the last phase of Ranger School, the jungle phase in Florida, on the second to last mission of Ranger School, when he was caught by an RI grazing on naturally growing berries. Grazing was against the rules, so he was recycled to day one of Ranger School. For two weeks I got to know Price. He was a funny guy who was always trying to get away with breaking the rules. He was deprived of food and sleep for sixty days, so he would sneak food out of the chow hall for nighttime eating or sneak out of the barracks at night to make phone calls.

When the next Ranger class started, I was ready to do it again. Day one started with the physical fitness test. I was last in line for the first physical test, push-ups. I handed my score card to the RI, got down on the ground, on the palms of my hands and on my knees, waiting for the test to begin. "Get ready. Get set. Begin." I started the push-up test and the RI counted my repetitions out loud.

"One, two, three—ten, ten, ten, ten."

I looked at him, wondering why he stayed at ten.

"Straighten your back, Ranger. Chest to the ground," he said.

I kept pushing, with my back straight, going down until my chest touched the earth.

"Ten, eleven, twelve, twelve, twelve—twelve."

The two minutes were up, and I failed. I was corralled into an area marked by white engineering tape. Price was there, with the look of defeat.

"I'm getting kicked out of the Regiment," he said.

"I'm getting kicked out of the Scout platoon," I told him.

"Maybe I'll end up in the 82nd and I'll see you."

"I hope you don't," I said to Price. "But if you do, I'll see you there. Take care, bro."

I returned to Fort Bragg as a failure. I walked onto the Scout platoon floor with my duffel bags and my rucksack, waiting for the ass chewing and the ridicule coming my way. It was nighttime, about 1900 hours, when I arrived at the barracks. I planned on getting in my room as quickly as possible, avoiding everyone until the morning, but I didn't have the key to my room.

A barracks room door was open down the hall and I could see the reflection of a TV program on the hallway floor and guys laughing. It was Sullivan's room. Sullivan earned his Ranger Tab before we deployed to Iraq. Sully and I were close, but I was ashamed of my failure and feared what Sully's reaction would be. Would he make fun of me? Would he insult me for failing? Was he in favor of me being kicked out of the platoon?

All these questions went through my mind as I approached his room. I stood outside his doorway and saw Sully, PFC Mealor, PFC Steel, PFC Grub, PFC Nick and PFC Kyle Amsberry. Mealor and Steel came to our platoon from B Co., after we returned from Fallujah, while Nick and Kyle, brothers who joined together, came from C Co. Kyle Amsberry and I would become best friends later. Grub came to us from A Co., and we graduated the same airborne class. Grubb was with the A Co. squad providing security for our Scout team during the home invasion.

I stood at the door for a few seconds before they noticed me. They all turned at the same time and saw me in the hallway, holding my bags. Sully got up, walked toward me, and gave me a brotherly hug. One after another, Steel, Mealor, and Grub hugged me and welcomed me back. Sully handed me a beer, looked me in the eyes, and said,

"It's statistics, brother. It's statistics."

"What do you mean?"

"Statistically, 60 percent of those who go to Ranger School will not graduate. You'll get it next time."

We drank and watched movies until 0100, on a work night, then Sully noticed I had my duffel bags in the hallway, outside his door.

"Why don't you put that in your room?"

"I don't have the key to my room. I turned the keys into Mac before I left."

"Then you can have my bed tonight. I'll sleep on the floor."

"What? No man. I'll sleep on the floor."

"Nah, that bed is making me soft while *hadjis* in Iraq are getting stronger."

I slept on Sully's bed while he slept on the floor.

The next day, I was called in by SSG Mac, Lt. O'Brian, and our new platoon sergeant, SFC Marengo. After I explained why I failed Ranger School, O'Brian asked me,

"Do you want to try it again?"

"Yes, sir."

"You know you'll have to go through PRC again, right?"

"Whatever it takes, sir."

They decided I could stay in the Scout platoon but, if I failed again, I was going to be removed from the platoon. For several days, wherever I was at Fort Bragg, I kept an eye out for Price, but I never saw him. *Maybe they let him stay in the Regiment*, I thought. Two weeks after my return to Bragg, when I was packing my bags for the next PRC, I started hearing rumors, more like gossip. I heard the SMU located Bin Laden in the mountains of Afghanistan, near the Pakistan border. We were going to deploy to help surround Bin Laden, who was protected by his fiercest and most loyal fighters, and kill him. Other rumors were we were going to parachute into Afghanistan and clear caves in a mountain region the Taliban made into their headquarters. I even heard most of us were expected to die on this mission.

Our brigade was now on DRF-1 and our bags were packed. We were ready to respond to any situation in the world and be there within eighteen hours of notification. I was drinking with the boys one weeknight, when our phones started ringing, almost simultaneously. I felt my phone vibrate in my pocket, so I answered.

"Is this Private Fernando Arroyo?"

"Yes, this is me."

"I'm Staff Sergeant Johnson. Red Corvette. I say again, Red Corvette."

"Roger, Staff Sergeant."

As I hung up my phone, I could hear multiple voices in the barracks hallway, shouting, "Red Corvette! F----n' Red Corvette!" Guys came out of their barracks rooms with cases of beer, and we drank a lot as we put on our desert camouflage and desert boots. I grabbed my deployment bag and headed to the arms room.

Within one hour, we were drunk, armed, and ready to deploy. We boarded cattle trucks that drove us to Green Ramp, at Pope Air Force base. We were surprised to see Delta Airlines aircraft on the tarmac. Before we boarded the planes to Afghanistan, we were gathered for a mission briefing. It turns out the reason we were going to Afghanistan was to provide additional security for the first free elections since the removal of the Taliban. I ate good food, ice cream, and watched movies the whole way. *This is how you're supposed go to war*, I thought, as I put the next spoon full of chocolate ice cream into my mouth. *God bless America!*

Several hours later, I was at Bagram Airfield, Afghanistan.

SSG Mish, Kyle Amsberry, and I were going with the 1st and 2nd Platoons from B Co. to a town called Zurmat, to meet with a team from the 3rd Special Forces Group, and a company of Afghan army soldiers, to provide security for the upcoming elections, and carry out missions in support of Operation Enduring Freedom. We flew on a CH-47 Chinook to Zurmat. I looked out the rear door of the Chinook and was in awe of the mountainous landscape. I thought, *Oh, s---! This is where the September 11 attacks were plotted.* Then I thought, *Oh, s---! This terrain is going to suck!* It was September 2004, and Afghanistan was cold and getting colder.

"Lord, I know I haven't talked to You like I should or lived my life the way I should. Forgive me for my sins, Lord. I ask that You protect me and my buddies on this deployment. I pray for Sarah, and that I will come home to her. I pray that she'll be the woman I marry. I pray for my family back home, that You would please protect them. In the name of Jesus Christ, I pray. Amen."

Chapter Twenty-Four

The Stan

I WAS SITTING in the back of a cargo Humvee and I was shivering. I was on a mission with B Co. 1st Platoon and the ODA team (Operational Detachment Alpha) from 3rd Group, to raid two villages about a quarter mile away from each other. The ODA and Afghan soldiers were going to go after one of the villages and we would attack the other. ODA intel discovered these villages were housing the Taliban and funding them by selling opium, which is processed to make heroin.

Kyle and I moved closer to each other in the back of the cargo Humvee, hoping our body heat would bring back the feeling in our faces, arms, and legs. The two-hour drive to the target village was painful, but we finally arrived. These villages were built like compounds, surrounded by thick mud walls as hard as stone. The walls were about fifteen feet high, with one fifteen-foot metal door, serving as the only entrance.

When we arrived, the ODA and Afghan soldiers separated from us toward their target village. I dismounted the Humvee and tried to run to the huge, red metal door, but my legs were numb. The best I could do was try to power walk, but even that was a struggle. As we stacked on either side of the door, I saw Weise, Cadena, and Viola running in place. Soon we were all running in place, trying to warm up before we entered the village. Once the combat engineers placed the explosive charge on the door, one of them yelled, "Fire in the hole, fire in the hole, fire in the hole!" The charge exploded and sparks flew as the huge doors swung open. Mish, Kyle, and I were tasked with clearing a mud hut closest to the gate, just past a courtyard, and establishing an overwatch position to provide cover for B Co.'s hut clearing.

I entered the courtyard and there was a fence protecting a small crop of vegetables to the right of the main door. The guys from 1st Platoon moved around the first building, which was the biggest and tallest, toward the six huts in the back. Our team, with some Air Force Tactical Air Control Party (TACP) guys, would clear the first building and provide sniper cover and close air support (CAS).

Kyle and I stacked to the right of the door. I was the number one man, the first man entering the building. I carried an M-4 with the M-203 grenade launcher, Kyle carried the M-4, but because I was more senior to Kyle, I was first. Mish turned the doorknob and pulled the door open, then I "button hooked" left into the room, clearing my corners, while Kyle went right and cleared his corners. When I could I said "Clear," and Mish and the TACPs entered the room. The room had nothing on the walls and no furniture. There was only a fireplace and a red Persian-style carpet.

"Where is the door into the next room?" said Mish. We were used to Fallujah, Iraq. In Fallujah the homes, although third world, were standard—we would enter a house and the room we entered had a door leading to the next room. Here, there was no door. Yet, from the outside of the hut, we could see there were more rooms. I surveyed the room and saw a small hole in the wall. I moved up to check it out.

"There's a tunnel," I said.

"What the f---?" Mish was confused.

"I'm going in."

"Do it."

I kneeled to look down the small hole. I pointed my weapon down the tunnel and saw it was about ten feet long and it led to another room that looked like a kitchen.

I could barely fit in the tunnel with all my gear, but I kept my weapon pointed into the next room as I crawled through. As I got closer to the end, the leg of a hoofed animal appeared. *Is there a horse in the kitchen?* I thought. As I got closer to the end of the tunnel, the animal uttered a bray and moved away. "It's a donkey!" I said in surprise. I crawled out and there was donkey poop, and a pile of onions in the corner of the room. I saw many things in combat, but that was the first and only time in my life that I've ever seen a donkey in a kitchen.

Once everyone made their way through the tunnel, we reached our overwatch position. I watched as 1st Platoon cleared the huts without any issues. Then I looked up at the sky, hoping to see some air support, but there was none. I looked over to my left at the two TACPs, and I asked them,

"Where is our air support?"

One of them said, "Look up." I looked again but I didn't see anything.

"There ain't s--- up there."

"Look closer."

I thought he was messing with me.

I looked again and I could see, far up above the clouds, two A-10 Thunderbolt aircraft, a.k.a. Warthogs, hovering overhead. Everyone loves the A-10 Warthog. It's a CAS airplane designed around a 30mm Gatling gun that can fire sixty-five rounds per second. We call it the Warthog because of the deep-sounding growl it makes when it fires the Gatling gun. The raid was a success. We captured some Taliban guys, some opium and hashish, then returned to Zurmat.

I was deployed to Afghanistan for two months. During those months, we spent most of our time carrying out counter IED missions, missions to kill or capture high-value targets, and counter mortar operations. During each combat mission, I felt the "normal" hypervigilance that comes with wandering the Afghan mountains at nighttime, with the looming threat of a Taliban encounter.

The Afghan elections were a success and we were heading home. I was looking forward to seeing my family and spending time with Sarah.

But my mind wasn't right.

Chapter Twenty-Five

Combat Neurosis

AFTER AFGHANISTAN, I returned to Fort Bragg. I woke up in my barracks room. The lights were on and I was on my bed looking up at the ceiling tiles. *How did I get here?* I wondered. I sat up slowly because my head was spinning. There was a weird smell in my room, like the smell of old food, so I looked around and saw a pool of vomit on the tile floor next to my bed. Then I felt a sudden jolt of panic and I jumped up and out of my bed. "Where's my weapon?" I looked under my bed and in my closet, but I couldn't find my weapon or any of my gear. I felt like my heart was going to jump out of my chest.

Then I remembered, "Oh, yeah. I'm back at Bragg." I sat back down on my bed for a few seconds, then I got up to find some cleaning supplies to deal with the mess I made. Army psychologist Brigadier General Loree Sutton once made an interesting observation: "We were not allowed to speak of the unseen wounds of war. We were not allowed to prepare for them." From day one, I had no idea how true this was.

Soon I was home for two weeks of vacation. I spent most of my time with Sarah. We made love and hung out every day, but she clearly felt something was wrong with me. She said I was "different." When I asked her what she meant, she said I seemed "bored." Sarah noticed I didn't want to go anywhere. I tried to avoid public places and when I was in a public place, I wasn't "with her."

Mentally, I was somewhere else.

I started noticing, like a song on repeat, I could hear machine gun fire, explosions, and radio chatter playing in my head. The only time it stopped was when I was alone with Sarah, and I could talk to her. I could hold her, look in her eyes, and feel her lips. That's when the recording stopped, or I should say paused. That's why I didn't want to go anywhere, but I didn't tell her. I didn't tell anyone, especially the guys I served with. After the two weeks were over, I hugged Sarah goodbye, waved farewell to my family, and flew back to Bragg. I was going back to PRC.

Chapter Twenty-Six

The Winter Ranger

IT WAS DÉJÀ VU at Towle Stadium, except it was cold and fewer men volunteered to try out for a slot in PRC. It was January 2005, and the cold temperatures made the journey, to and through Ranger School, more difficult. I passed all the same tests, and I was one of fifty to go to PRC. We did all the same torturous events, running five miles in the sand at a five-minute-thirty-second-per-mile pace, enduring a twelve-mile road march, practicing land navigation and running up and down the hill. Morning temperatures were below freezing, and we were soaked in sweat from all the exercise. I constantly saw steam rising from my body.

The last week consisted of graded patrols and the temperatures in the night went as low as 5 degrees below zero. On one such cold and miserable night, the RIs had us make a circle perimeter in the woods, next to a fire break. Then they told us to lay prone, in teams of two. After about five minutes of lying on the freezing ground, I began to shiver. Across the fire break, about twenty-five meters from our position, I could see two Humvees and four RIs gathering wood for a fire. They made a big fire and I could see their smiling faces as they enjoyed the warmth of the flames. Then, from back of one of the Humvees, the RIs opened a green plastic container, allowing steam to escape into the cold night. It was soup. The RIs were drinking hot soup in their canteen cups by the fire.

My Ranger buddy was a member of the 3rd Special Forces Group, and I saw him grinding his body in the earth to create heat. He turned over to me and said,

"Hey, Arroyo."

"What's up?"

"Grind on me, dude."

"What?"

"Grind on me, bro. It's freezing. I can't feel my face."

We were lying next to each other, spooning, with his back to my front, and I started grinding my body on his. This may sound weird, but when it's negative five degrees and you're soaking wet, your life is in danger.

Two of the Ranger instructors left the comfort of the fire and walked over to our perimeter, each holding their canteen cup with hot soup.

"Listen up, Rangers," the RI said, and then paused to sip on his hot soup. "Damn, that's good soup." Then he continued, "This training is not for everyone. Most of you will not make it through Ranger School. It's statistics, men. Some of you are already doubting yourselves and wondering if you're gonna make it. You're not! If you want to quit now, there will be no questions asked, and there will be no judgment. We will give you soup, a blanket, and let you enjoy the fire. We'll take you back to camp, let you pack your things and go."

Immediately, one student stood, picked up his gear, walked over to the RIs and said, "I quit." The platoon erupted, "No! Don't do it, man! You'll regret this for the rest of your life!"

"Do you quit?" the RI asked.

"Yes, I quit."

I watched, as I shivered uncontrollably on the ground, while the student who quit walked with the RIs to the fire. He was given a hearty serving of soup and a blanket, as the RIs were having a casual conversation with him. After a few minutes, two more students got up and were given the same treatment. This is while I was grinding my face, my arms, and my legs on my Ranger buddy. Eventually, we all started yelling at the quitters, letting them know they were scumbags. The RIs let us run our mouths for a few minutes and even laughed as they listened to the things we were saying. The three quitters were loaded on a Humvee and driven back to camp.

I don't know how long we were left to freeze on the ground, but the RIs came over and said, "Good job, men. Never quit." They walked us over to the fire, gave us soup, and then returned us to the warmth of the camp barracks. If the three men who quit would have just waited a few more minutes, they would have enjoyed all the same comforts, in victory. Twenty of us made it to graduation. Now I was on my way to Ranger School, again.

Chapter Twenty-Seven

Agoge

I WAS BACK at Fort Benning, Georgia, for my second attempt at Ranger School. Just like the first time, I watched as men who appeared to be physically stronger than me, broke down and quit. I took it one day at a time, and one event at a time. I passed the physical fitness test and the swim test. I endured the smoke sessions throughout the day and the hours of combatives in the pit. The next day was land navigation. I trusted my pace count and found all my points with enough time to take a nap. I endured the freezing muddy waters of the legendary Malvesti Obstacle Course, jumping water so cold I felt my skin burning. I passed the water confidence course, walking on a thirty-foot-high beam, and zip-lining into Victory Pond from sixty feet high. Every day ended with hours of combatives. Within the first week, over 100 students quit.

To help me stay positive, I started impersonating the RIs, which is something people tell me I'm good at. I would yell, "Hey, Ranger!" and start barking orders in the same voice as an RI, and students would get scared. Most of them laughed but one student didn't like it. His name was Papp (Doc Papps), from the 75th Ranger Regiment. He hated me for my impressions. He often threatened to punch me in the face, but I welcomed it. I kept scaring him on purpose, just to get a reaction. He was pissed.

I was in the chow hall for lunch, and an RI approached me.

"Hey, Ranger!" I looked up with food in my mouth since we were given about one minute to finish our meals, so I quickly swallowed my food.

"Sergeant?" I don't know why I was surprised, but it was SSG Eton.

"What happened last time you were here?"

"I failed land nav, Sergeant."

"Well, you're past that now. Tomorrow is the road march. Don't quit!"

"Yes, Sergeant. I won't." SSG Eton walked away.

Now that the RAP week (Ranger assessment phase) was over, we were headed to Camp Rogers, on foot. It is a sixteen-mile road march, over uneven and sandy terrain. I made the decision that morning to not eat my MRE (meal ready to eat) because I feared having to poop during the march, which would disqualify me from training. I watched guys break down and quit during those sixteen miles. I was determined to make it to Camp Rogers, and I kept pushing myself, putting one foot in front of the other. It was mile fifteen, with one more to go, and my vision started to blur. I couldn't see out of my right eye, but I kept moving. *I have to make it*, I said to myself.

A Ranger instructor grabbed my arm. I looked to him, surprised he put his hands on me. "Come on, Ranger. You need to see the medic." I guess he could tell I wasn't normal. He walked me over to the Army ambulance and three medics quickly started taking my gear off. I was told to lie down on a litter, and they started to unfasten my pants.

"Hey, what the f--- are you doing?"

"Relax, we need to take your core temperature."

"What?"

"You're gonna feel a sting."

"Huh?"

I felt the sting of a thermometer going up my butthole. It was cold and uncomfortable, and it lasted a few seconds. "You're good. You just need glucose." I was given a small white tube of glucose to eat, and I was told to return to training. I walked up to the RI who took me to the ambulance.

"Where do I go, Sergeant?" I felt defeated because I thought that I was going to be recycled.

"You feeling better, Ranger?"

"Yes, Sergeant."

"Alright, get back with your company. You're good to go."

It turns out I was past the sixteen-mile point when the RI grabbed me. I think he waited for me to finish before he grabbed me for medical attention.

In three weeks at Camp Darby, I learned how to plan, lead, and conduct ambushes, raids, and recon operations. I was given two MREs to be eaten as one meal a day, every twenty-four hours, and I lost thirty pounds in three weeks. I passed my graded patrols at Darby and I moved on to the mountain phase.

In that phase we were given two meals a day for the first week. I learned military mountaineering, knot tying, and mountain climbing. On the first of ten days of patrols in the Appalachian Mountains of Dahlonega, Georgia, I experienced a new level of suffering I never thought possible. The cold night at PRC paled in comparison to the snowstorms, hail, and rain of the mountain phase. The second day of graded patrols, we only slept about twenty minutes. An officer who had to recycle the mountain phase, walked up to the three RIs in the center of the patrol base.

"I can't do this, Sergeant. I quit."

"Negative. Get your gear and get back to your fighting position, Ranger."

"I can't. I can't do this anymore. I quit." The officer had tears rolling down his cheeks as we all watched in silence.

"Alright, get in the truck."

We were carrying over 100 pounds of gear: ropes, harnesses, ammo, machine guns, rifles, carabiners, radios, batteries, and much more. The slippery mountain terrain paired with food and sleep deprivation meant we were slipping and falling on rocks all the time. I was psychologically drained. By the tenth day, every time I fell, I kind of wished a bone would break, so I could have a legitimate reason to stop, but it never happened.

On the last day, we were about to find out if we met the standards to move on to the jungle phase in Florida. I was a zombie standing in formation, watching men collapse. Yes, they literally collapsed. By then our brains were shutting down from the lack of sleep. An RI came out from the C Co. building and shouted,

"Listen up, Rangers! If I call your name, come around to the opposite side of the building. Leave your gear where it is."

He read off several names, about twenty, then I heard,

"Arroyo!"

"Here, Sergeant."

My name was among those called, and I knew what this meant. I failed. I joined the group whose names were called and we all looked at each other with wide eyes, knowing we failed. The question in everyone's mind was, *Would I do this again?*

"Listen up, Rangers. You're going to report to the First Sergeant. You will knock on his door three times, and wait for the command of, 'enter,' then you will enter his office, stand in front of his desk and present arms. You will state your name and say,

"'Reporting as ordered, First Sergeant.' Do you understand?"

"Yes, Sergeant."

Do I want to do this again? I thought, as I waited to see the First Sergeant. I watched as one after another, students walked out of the First Sergeant's office either as recycles or quitters. It was my turn. I knocked on the door three times and he said, "Enter."

I walked in, saluted, reported as ordered, and he told me to "Relax." The First Sergeant told me the RIs who graded me thought I wasn't fast enough on calling the 9-line medevac when a student was wounded, and I lost control of the platoon during my graded patrol when we were taking indirect fire.

"Ranger, you have three options. Option one is day-one recycle, where you will go back to Fort Benning and repeat the entire first phase before returning to the mountains. The second option is 'quit.' You can pack your bags and put this all behind you, Ranger. The last option is to recycle the mountain phase and wait one week for the next class to arrive. What's it gonna be, Ranger?"

My body wanted me to quit. I was hungry, exhausted, physically, and mentally, and all I wanted was to go away to anywhere but here. I remembered SSG Eton and our conversation in the chow hall when he told me, "Don't quit." I looked at the First Sergeant and I opened my mouth, saying,

"First Sergeant, I choose to recycle the mountain phase."

"That's what I'm talkin' about, Ranger! Never quit!"

I was now a recycle.

Chapter Twenty-Eight

The Care Package

I WAS A recycle student in the Ranger School, alongside several others. I was assigned a bed and I walked into the barracks and started putting my gear in a wall locker, when I heard, "Hell no!"

I looked behind me and it was Papps. He was a short white guy, about five feet, five inches tall, and he was pissed. Not only did Papps hate me, but he was also assigned the bed next to me. For the next week, Papps and I were going to be neighbors.

"Hey, buddy," I said to him with a smile on my face.

"F--- you!" He looked at me like he was deciding whether or not to punch me in the face.

"Aw, come on, Pappy. Let's be friends."

"F--- you, and don't call me Pappy, you ass----!"

I finished putting my gear in my locker and laid on my bunk. Papp sat on his bunk, about two feet away from me, facing me. He noticed I limped back to my bunk and I was in pain. My knees were swollen, filled with fluid, and my feet were swollen. While I was lying in bed groaning with pain, I looked over at Papp and smiled. He had a look on his face like I was the one who recycled him. Despite the pain on my knees, I managed to smile again.

"We're gonna be best friends before this is over," I told him.

"Negative!" Papp said with a look of disgust on his face.

"Are you Irish?" I asked.

"Yeah, I'm Irish. What the f--- is it to you?"

"Haha! Now I know why you're angry."

"I'm mad because I have to sleep next to your dumbass."

"No, that's not why. You wanna know why you're angry?"

"Why am I angry?"

"Because you have the curse of the Irish. You have a small d---, and a big liver." Papps tried not to laugh but he couldn't help it. We laughed until we had tears in our eyes.

"What unit are you with?"

"Headquarters, 75th Ranger Regiment," he said, with some pride.

"What do you do in the Regiment?"

"I'm a combat medic. What about you? What unit are you with? What do you do?"

"I'm with the greatest unit in the armed forces, the 82nd Airborne Division. I'm a grunt."

Papps laughed when I said that and then he started giving me medical advice. He told me to elevate my feet and helped me do it. Throughout my week as a recycle, Papps and I became good friends. He made sure I was up for every meal. Sometimes we stole food from the chow hall, even saving it for each other if one of us missed the opportunity.

One day, all the recycles were waiting to eat outside the chow hall and we were sharing war stories. I mentioned I served in Zurmat, Afghanistan, and someone chimed in.

"Who said they were in Zurmat!?"

"I was in Zurmat! Why?"

"When were you there?"

"From September '04 to November '04."

"I was there too. Who were you with?"

"82nd Airborne. You?"

"3rd Group."

His name was Ken and we were unaware being on the same base in Zurmat at the same time. We were on several raids, including the "donkey in the kitchen raid." With him was Quintana, from the 7th Special Forces Group CIF Team (Commanders In-extremis Force), a direct action team from the Green Berets. We became friends and enjoyed sharing stories from Zurmat. I told him about smoking weed with Kyle, and he told me about missions I was unaware of. His 3rd Group was doing things in the shadows the 82nd couldn't be told about.

We went to church one day at a small white chapel. I heard stories about their being the "snake handling" type Christians. I never saw them dancing with snakes as was rumored, but I was able to pray. I asked God for forgiveness of my sins and I knew in my heart I was doing the wrong things. I was sleeping with Sarah, I was relying on my own strength, and I believed being recycled was God's way of waking me up. He was reminding me I should rely on Him and not my own strength.

That Sunday I prayed, "Lord, help me through this training. I can't do it without You."

Every evening, Papp, Quintana, Ken, and I went out at night to dumpster dive. We were starving from only eating one meal a day for the last twenty-something days, and the three meals a day at the chow hall weren't enough. I remember going into a dumpster and finding a half-eaten sandwich. We shared it. We were brothers, so we looked out for each other.

One morning I was in the recycle barracks and everyone started yelling my name.

"What's up?"

"An RI is looking for you. He's outside," Papp told me.

I walked outside the barracks and there was SSG Mac, wearing a black shirt with a gold Ranger Tab, BDUs, and jungle boots.

"Hey, spic. What happened?" I was glad to see him. Mac and I went through hell and back and now he was an RI in the mountain phase.

"I'm good, Sergeant. How are you?"

"I'm alright. You're coming to A Co., that's where I'm at. Don't mess this up."

"I won't, Sergeant. Oh, by the way, I lost my helmet."

"What?! I just got done telling all the RIs how you're a squared-away and a bad-ass dude. What the hell is wrong with you?"

"Sorry, Sergeant, but I was half asleep and I don't know where it is."

Mac got me a new helmet and I began to feel less depressed.

The next class started, and I was told by the RIs to help teach the students how to tie the ten different knots we learned. I was standing in the middle of a rope corral where everyone practiced their knot tying, when someone asked me for help.

I looked up and it was Price, my recycle buddy from the first time I went through Ranger School.

"Ha! What's up, Price?" But I noticed his name tape read "Pierce."

"Pierce?"

"Don't worry about it. Some dude named Pierce quit in Darby, so I stole some of his uniforms."

Price hadn't changed. He was still the conniving Ranger who always looked to get away with things. But he was my buddy from 2/75 Rec, and I was happy to see him. My morale kept improving and I looked up at the sky, "Thank You, Lord."

Then I heard, "Hey, buster!" The voice was familiar . . . *could it be?* It was Kyle Amsberry! He looked about thirty pounds lighter, and his front tooth was chipped. He told me he was hallucinating from the sleep deprivation in Darby, and he thought his flashlight was a chocolate brownie. When he bit his flashlight, his tooth broke. This was common, and I met a few guys with chipped teeth throughout my time at Ranger School.

Price, Papp, and I were in the same company, and we helped each other out through the mountain phase. I saw Kyle, who was in C Co., in passing, but seeing my Scout brother was encouraging. One day, we were in the planning bay, a hut made of plywood, where we had classes during the first week on mountain warfare tactics. Students drew their unit's insignia, using chalk, and wrote the names of their classmates from the same unit.

I saw an 82nd Airborne drawing with the names of the Scout platoon members from when I first arrived at the unit. I saw Howerton, Birchfield, Kline, Knouse, Sullivan, and several others. I added mine and Kyle's name to the list. I looked at the front of the bay and saw, above the chalk board, a huge Ranger Regiment scroll, with the names of several Regiment guys. On it was my buddy Norris, from basic training, Elijah, and Pat Tillman. Elijah, who was my battle buddy, was Pat Tillman's Ranger buddy. They went through the school together, so I knew Pat Tillman was in good hands.

I passed my patrols in the mountains and made it to the jungle phase in Florida. Florida was the final stretch. We were given one meal a day from the beginning. The previous phases allowed us to eat twice during the first week, but Florida was the last test of our fortitude. Price acquired several MREs and let me have some crackers, peanut butter, and jelly, which was awesome.

I learned survival training. I killed a chicken by ripping its head off by using the groove of my jungle boot to trap the chicken's neck and then pulling the chicken by the legs, ripping its head off. Then I made chicken soup, I learned how to make rope bridges to cross rivers, how to call CAS, and I learned river operations.

When the first week of training was over, we parachuted into a landing zone and started our ten-day jungle warfare training. I passed my patrol as the platoon sergeant on a mission called, "The Weaver," which was the second to last mission of Ranger School. If I didn't get hurt or bitten by a snake, I was set to graduate.

It was time for the final mission. We were going to attack the last enemy stronghold, located at Santa Rosa Island. The plan was to infiltrate the coast by zodiac boats, land on the shore, set up the support by fire and assault team positions, before raiding the enemy compound that looked like a big warehouse building. Unfortunately, the weather report changed our plans. There was a storm coming, making an amphibious assault too risky. Instead, we boarded five-ton trucks and drove to Santa Rosa Island, just a few miles away from the objective, and walked to our target. I was a part of the support by fire team, serving as the assistant gunner (AG) of an M-240B machine gun team.

Under the cover of the night, we set up our three machine gun teams on a sand berm overlooking the objective. Once the assault teams were ready, we received the call over the radio to begin firing. The machine gun fire was deafening, as I kept connecting belt after belt of 7.62 ammo, feeding the machine gun to sustain fire. I was all smiles as I watched the assault team do their job, knowing I was just a few minutes away from being done with the final mission and on my way to being awarded my Ranger Tab.

"Index!" I heard the call over the radio signaling the end of the final mission. My buddies and I hugged, telling each other, "We made it."

A couple of days after the final mission, we returned to Fort Benning, Georgia, for our graduation ceremony at Victory Pond, where it all began. Price, Kyle, and I posed for our Ranger School graduation photo, Ranger School Class 06-05 (class six of 2005). We turned in our gear and hung out in the same gravel-covered formation area where we started. I was sleeping on the gravel when I heard my name.

"Ranger Arroyo!" my entire class echoed the command but, my buddy, Doc Papps came to wake me up so I wouldn't get in trouble. I ran over to a group of RIs and Sergeant Eton was there.

"Yes, Sergeant," I said at the position of parade rest.

"I heard you recycled mountain phase."

"Yes, Sergeant," I smiled because he was tracking my progress.

"You didn't quit."

"No, Sergeant. I'm a man of my word."

"Good job. Welcome to the brotherhood. Rangers Lead the Way!"

I graduated Ranger School and I was disappointed no one showed up to my graduation. Kyle's mother flew down from Arizona to pin the Ranger Tab on his shoulder. I looked around, like I did during every time I returned from combat, and saw families together, celebrating. No one was there for me, so I pinned my Ranger Tab on my own left shoulder. Kyle called me over and he introduced me to his mother. He asked if anyone was here for me, and I shook my head, no. He saw my tab was crooked, so he straightened it out while his mom took a picture of us.

"Arroyo!" I looked around but at first I didn't see anyone.

"Arroyo!" Then I saw it was Eggy and SSG Herbst. They were at Pathfinder School and skipped their lunch break to be there for Kyle and me. Eggy gave me a big hug and congratulated me. Eggy and I were at Ranger School the first time I went. He made it through and was always supportive of me. He, like Sully, Knouse, and Mac, were always encouraging me. I was one of them, in the fullest sense. We shared a brotherhood spirit less than 1 percent of servicemen would ever experience. Airborne! All the Way! Rangers Lead the Way!

Chapter Twenty-Nine

Falling

I WAS FEELING great after Ranger School, and I went home to Bell Gardens and saw Sarah. We made love and had fun going to the beach and exploring different local attractions. I listened to her worries—she tried to explain to me how I seemed somehow closed off, so I tried to be more outgoing. I had one year of service left in the Army and we talked about our future together. The plan was in August of 2006, I would get out of the Army, join the Los Angeles Police Department, buy a house, get married, have kids, and we would live happily ever after.

My two weeks with Sarah filled me with hope for the future. With that buoying my spirits, I returned to Fort Bragg, ready to lead troops in the Scout platoon. I left for Ranger School with the rank of Private First Class, but I was promoted to the rank of Corporal upon my return. I was now the Hawk 3, Team 3 Assistant Team Leader (ATL) serving under SSG Taylor. Taylor took SSG Mac's place, and my life was going to be great.

At the time, I wasn't aware of an old Yiddish proverb: "Man plans, God laughs."

I led training exercises with the more senior Scouts. McGuire, Howerton, Martin, and others, looked at me as their equal. I served with them in combat and I passed the test of Ranger School, so I was officially one of them. Kyle and I were on the same team, and it was an incredible experience to plan and execute training exercises with him. His brother Nick and Seiler—a.k.a Squeegee, a.k.a. Sloppy—graduated

Ranger School after Kyle and I, and we all worked together. We were great friends.

First Sergeant Lopez called me into his office one day. "Good job at Ranger School. Go ahead and put in a packet for Jumpmaster School, Sniper School, Pathfinder School and Air Assault School, and the Special Operations Combat Diver Course."

"Yes, First Sergeant. I will do that." I felt great to be a Ranger School grad and have many other training opportunities.

"Before you apply for all these schools, go ahead and talk to reenlistment and let's get you another contract."

"I don't plan on reenlisting, First Sergeant." I thought about my plans with Sarah. I was going to get out, join the LAPD, marry her, have kids, and live happily ever after.

"What?"

"I don't plan on staying in the Army, First Sergeant."

"Well, being in the Scout platoon is a privileged position. If you're not staying in, then you need to go back to where you came from."

"First Sergeant, I was hoping to finish my time with my brothers in the Scouts."

"Negative. If you don't reenlist, you're going back to B Co. 1st Platoon."

"I'm not reenlisting, First Sergeant."

"Okay. Go back to the Scouts and I'll keep you posted."

"Yes, First Sergeant."

The next day, McGuire yelled my name down the barracks hallway. "Arroyo!"

"Yes, Staff Sergeant McGuire!"

"Pack your bags, brother." He looked disappointed. McGuire and I went through several battles together, including my first fire fight in the swamps of Fallujah.

"You're going back to B Co. I'll walk you over. You have one hour to pack your bags, per First Sergeant Lopez."

I packed up and McGuire walked me to the B Co. 1SG Dobbs's office. He knocked on the door three times. The 1SG said, "Enter!"

"First Sergeant, Staff Sergeant McGuire, reporting as ordered."

"Yes, you're bringing me the new B Co. paratrooper.

"Yes, First Sergeant."

"Okay, thanks, Staff Sergeant. You're dismissed."

With that, McGuire turned to me and he whispered, "Sorry, brother," as he walked out of the office.

"So, I remember you from the E-5 board."

"Yes, First Sergeant."

"Relax." I could tell 1SG Dobbs was different. He was the only 1SG in our battalion without a Ranger Tab, yet he had the reputation for being the best 1SG in our battalion. I worked so hard for the Ranger Tab, and here was a 1SG who didn't earn the Tab, telling me what to do.

First Sergeant Dobbs spoke to me like no other 1SG ever did. He talked to me like I was human. He was a polite man, with a calm demeanor, which demonstrated the highest level of professionalism. My first day speaking to 1SG Dobbs, I learned a lesson that would follow me the rest of my life. "Meet them where they are."

Dobbs knew I didn't want to leave the Scout platoon; he knew I was feeling betrayed, and he knew I didn't want to return to B Co. He made it clear to me he knew all these things, and he also made it clear he was happy to have me join the team.

So I was back where I started three years earlier, and I was a team leader in third squad. There were changes happening in the 82nd Airborne Division to adapt to the war on terror. The 3rd Battalion, 505th Parachute Infantry Regiment was disbanded. We received several paratroopers from their battalion. SPC Andrew Renne, PFC Josh Hanson, SPC Jason Radamacher, and SSG Young joined 3rd squad. I was the alpha team leader and SSG Young was my new squad leader. We went to JRTC (Joint Readiness Training Center) and we exchanged tactics and information. I had less than one year before I got out of the Army in August 2006, but I was still doing my best for the remainder of my time.

Before I left for JRTC, I received a letter from the 82nd Airborne Division. The letter informed me I was designated "stop-loss." That meant my unit was set to deploy to Iraq in August and the Division could not afford to lose me. So I was going to have to stay in my unit for an extra year of service in Iraq, and possibly longer.

At that point I was infuriated with the Army. I had plans for being with Sarah, but my future was being placed on hold. I called her and told her I was stop-loss. I told her I would deploy to Iraq for a year or longer, in August.

She was angry, too, and at first she didn't know what to say. Then she told me, "No. I can't wait. I just can't put my life on hold for you again. I think we should both move on."

"What? Our plans are delayed but we can still be together. We'll be together later than we planned, but we'll still be together."

"Fernando, I'm sorry. I can't do this. I need to move on. Take care of yourself."

She was crying as she hung up the phone.

So that was it. I was kicked out of the Scout platoon, I was stop-loss, and the woman I loved was leaving me. I went from feeling invincible to feeling completely broken. There was only one person to blame for all of this, and it was God. God took her away from me, God kept me from getting out of the Army, and God was making me feel miserable.

I was angry with God, and meanwhile I had to train for war.

JRTC, in Fort Polk, Louisiana, gave our platoon an opportunity to get to know each other and train for the upcoming fight. SSG Young and I worked together to get our squad up to speed. We cleared rooms, using ladders, flash-bangs, explosives, and simulation rounds. We trained for hours for several days, and then we were tasked with taking down an enemy compound, using live fire.

A few days later we were lined up beside a landing zone (LZ) waiting for the helicopters. When I heard the rotors, I looked above the wood line and I saw several Blackhawks and Apaches. We loaded up. The helicopters traveled low—NOE (nap of the earth)—and we were inserted to an LZ where pop-up targets became visible, and the door gunners opened fire.

We headed into the wood line and I heard a radio call from Hawk 1 Romeo, saying their team was in position. We ran into a trench and used it as cover. Once we were all in place, 1st, 2nd, and 3rd platoon machine gun teams began to fire. Twenty-eight M-240B machine guns opened fire, too, killing several of the enemy personnel targets. I was in the trench by the breach point when the combat engineers ran to the gate with a Bangalore.

"Fire in the hole! Fire in the hole! Fire in the hole!"

When the explosion went off, I saw all the new guys—Rene, Hanson, and Rademacher—flinch. They were surprised by the explosion, but SGT Cadena, SSG Young, SGT Horan, and I didn't even blink. We looked at the new guys without expression, as none of us were surprised by this kind of thing anymore. We all had two to four combat deployments under our belt. When 2nd Platoon moved up to enter the compound, we flipped them off yelling, "2nd Platoon sucks!" and they flipped us the bird as they were moving.

We eventually made our way into the compound and cleared a three-story building. The targets in the building were dummies that fell when we shot them, and they would also record where they were shot to provide our commanders with a report on our unit's level of marksmanship. When we finished clearing the building, I stood in a room by myself and I thought about my future. I felt alone. I was afraid of what the future had in store, and still in shock over how my plans fell apart. And now I was stop-loss. I lost the woman I loved, the career I wanted was on hold, and I was probably going to die in Iraq.

Time flew by and the month of August arrived. August 20, 2006, was the day I was supposed to leave the Army, but that wasn't going to happen. Instead, I had my bags packed and I was ready to go to Iraq for the second time for my third combat deployment. I looked through the contacts in my cell phone and I didn't know who to call before I left for war, and that's when Sarah called me.

"Hello."

"Hey, Fernando!"

"Who is this?"

"What? You don't remember me?"

"Sarah?"

"Yeah! It's me. How are you?"

Sarah had started dating another guy about three weeks after she broke up with me. And now she was calling me because that guy cheated on her. She was heartbroken and told me she'd made a mistake when she left me. I was a good guy, she said, and she wanted to see me again.

I told her I was in the middle of packing my bags to go to Iraq and that I didn't have time to talk.

"I'm sorry for hurting you, Fernando. And I want to keep in touch . . ."

I was seriously pissed off with this girl for breaking my heart and then coming back to me after somebody else broke hers. I figured I was her back-up plan.

I told her I had to go. I said goodbye, and Sarah started crying.

"I'm sorry, Fernando. I'm so sorry for hurting you."

I told her goodbye and hung up the phone. I was so angry—I smashed my phone on the barracks floor and stomped it until it didn't work anymore.

I was ready to die. I was sure this deployment was the final stretch of my life, and I would be killed. I thought God wanted me dead, so I started to mentally prepare myself for dying in combat.

Chapter Thirty

The Surge

I WAS BACK in Iraq for my third combat tour. It was "The Surge" and General Petraeus was the commander of forces in Iraq. I felt the familiar bump as the Chinook touched down on the tarmac of the helicopter runway at Forward Operating Base Summerall. We were relieving the 187th Infantry Regiment, Rakkasans, of the 101st Airborne Division.

The tarmac was in front of the battalion headquarters building and I noticed three concrete Jersey barriers turned into memorials. On them were chiseled the names of the fallen soldiers of the 187th Infantry Regiment. There were more than fifteen names recorded there. First Sergeant Dobbs and I read their names as helicopters kept landing, dropping off more of our men.

"This is going to be a tough deployment," 1SG Dobbs said. "May God protect us."

He was so right. The following fifteen months proved to be some of the most difficult days of my life.

Chapter Thirty-One

The Fallen

CPL NICHOLAS A. ARVANITIS
KIA 06 October 2006, Bayji, Iraq

I was following the sound of music echoing through the barracks hallway, but I was so drunk I could barely put one foot in front of the other. Someone was listening to "Iron Man" by Black Sabbath while playing along with his electric guitar. The sound was hypnotic, and I wanted to know who was playing it. I held my beer with my left hand, and I used my right hand on the wall to keep myself from falling. I had to close one eye so I could stop seeing double and make my way down the Charlie Company barracks hallway. The sound of the guitar grew louder with every step. I made it to the room and I walked in as a young, blond, green-eyed, kid rocked out. I didn't know him, but he didn't seem to care as I walked into his room, sat on his couch, and listened to him play. He smiled and continued to bang his head as he slayed every note with his axe.

"What's up, man?" he said to me after the song finished and he turned down the music.

"I heard you rocking out and I wanted to see who it was." I wondered if he even understood what I was saying because I was most likely slurring my words.

"You're Knouse's friend, huh? You're a Scout. I've seen you hanging out with Knouse and Sullivan."

"Yeah, they're my Scout buddies. My name's Arroyo." I would have stretched out my hand to shake his, but I was so drunk it would have been a struggle to get off his couch.

"I'm Nicholas Arvanitis, but everyone calls me RV."

SGT Sullivan, SGT Knouse, SGT Holtzclaw (Claw), and SGT Sigua stormed in the room, each holding two beers, one in each hand.

"Arroyo, what the hell happened?" asked Knouse with a look of concern on his face.

"What do you mean?"

"We were in Bugger's (SGT Bougere) room and you disappeared. We were walking around the barracks looking for you."

"So I heard the guitar so I followed the sound."

Knouse, Sully, and Claw were relieved to have found me. Sigua laughed at the three of them, "You guys were about to cry. Like you were looking for a lost puppy, haha!"

Knouse sat next to me on the couch and put one arm around me. "I f------' love this guy." Then Knouse looked to RV and shouted at the top of his lungs, "Play something RV!" With that, RV turned up the music to a deafening level, and played his guitar to Black Sabbath's "Paranoid" as we all banged our heads to the music—except for Sully. Sully kept it gangster.

Only later, when I learned about RV's death did I reflect on General George Patton's words, "It is foolish and wrong to mourn the men who died. Rather we should thank God that such men lived."

I was standing under the hot desert sun in a military formation in front of our battalion headquarters building, in Bayji, Iraq. I was staring at a rifle, placed upside down on a wooden box, with RV's dog tags, boots, and his photograph.

RV was outside the wire at the Bayji Joint Security Station (JSS) when he carried his machine gun up into a guard tower because the Iraqi soldiers were too afraid to guard their own patrol base, which placed both Iraqi and American troops in danger. While guarding that base, RV's fellow soldiers heard a single gunshot. The sergeant in charge tried contacting RV over the radio, but there was no response. The platoon medic ran to the guard tower RV was manning and climbed up the ladder. He shouted, "RV! . . . RV!" There was no response. The medic reached the top of the twenty-foot guard tower. There he found RV lifeless on the floor. He was shot in the head by a sniper.

That day, I saw the toughest men in the world shed tears for our brother. I stood at attention as I tried to fight back my own tears. First Sergeant Green walked to the front of the Charlie Company formation facing RV's photo. He stood at attention, faced his men, and he gave the command, "Company! Attention!" C Co. snapped to.

"Sergeant Sullivan!"

"Here, First Sergeant!"

"Specialist Alzate!"

"Here, First Sergeant!"

"Sergeant Holtzclaw!"

"Here, First Sergeant!"

"Corporal Arvanitis!"

There was no response.

Again, 1SG Green shouted, "Corporal Arvanitis!" with no answer.

"Corporal Nicholas A. Arvanitis!"

The silence hung in the air.

"Present, arms!" The entire battalion saluted RV as the rifles fired in the three-volley salute. I continued to hold back my tears as the rifles finished firing in sequence, but the moment "Taps" was played I broke down.

Following the ceremony, I approached the wooden box with the photo of RV, his rifle, and his dog tags. I stood at attention, looked down at his photo, and saluted. Through my tears I could make out RV's smile. It was the same smile I saw when I entered his room and we rocked out. I brought down my hand and walked away.

SFC TONY L. KNIER
KIA 28 October 2006, Bayji, Iraq

On October 28, 2006, our battalion suffered another loss.

The D Co. platoon was tasked with securing a construction site where an Iraqi army patrol base was being built. This required them to drive off the road and into the sand, and in the sand insurgents placed an anti-tank landmine. They observed our movement patterns closely, looking for any way to kill us. Since we were rotating platoons to secure the construction site, those enemies figured out our daily guard rotations and where the Humvees usually traveled.

When the Humvee left the road and drove into the sand, the front passenger tire hit the landmine, killing the platoon sergeant, SFC Tony Knier.

Inside the Humvee, sitting behind SFC Knier was the medic, who was blown out of the Humvee and was temporarily unconscious. After a few seconds, when he came to, he got up and ran toward the shattered vehicle. Although he was wounded, covered in blood, he ignored his own injuries and began to treat SFC Knier. The sergeant suffered severe head trauma. He was transferred to another Humvee and rushed back to base for further medical treatment, but he died on the way.

SFC Knier was loved and respected by his men and all the paratroopers in our battalion. He was a Ranger School graduate and a jumpmaster, a man who pushed himself to his physical and mental limits. He did the same for his soldiers, bringing out the best in them. He had the reputation of being the finest platoon sergeant in D Co., and now his men had to fight on without him. Sadder still, he was also a husband, and the father of two beautiful babies.

CSM DONOVAN E. WATTS
KIA 21 November 2006, Bayji, Iraq

After Ranger School, I was sent to a promotional meeting that would elevate me to the rank of sergeant. All eyes were on me as I stood at attention in the presence of all five First Sergeants from our battalion. They sat behind a table in the B Co. meeting room, and in the middle, with 1SGs to his left and to his right, was battalion Command Sergeant Major Donovan E. Watts.

Watts was a patient man, and a thinking man with a thousand-yard stare. I never heard him scream in anger but, with a calm voice, he was direct and to the point, and he always had a smile. I never met a man who could so completely command a room with his presence, intimidating every alpha male—even while smiling—until I met him. The brightness of his smile was intensified by his black skin. But now, sitting between his 1SGs, he was not smiling.

I stood at attention wearing my Class A uniform. It took me an entire day to shine my jump boots, place every ribbon in its proper order, with just the right spacing. I presented arms, saluting CSM Watts. I said, "Corporal Fernando Arroyo reporting to the promotion board, as ordered."

All the 1SGs laughed at me and began to critique my uniform. "You look like s---, Arroyo," said one 1SG. "Are those ribbons even in the right order?" said another. All the while CSM Watts was silent. Then, remaining seated CSM Watts saluted me and said, in a calm voice, "Take a seat."

I sat with my back straight and my hands on my lap. I tried not to look any of the men in the eyes, thinking they might take it as a challenge to their authority and find reason to punish me with push-ups and an ear full of profanities.

"Let me hear your bio," said the CSM. So I briefly shared my life story, including my short-term and long-term goals. When I was finished, the room was silent. CSM Watts was just studying me with that stare of his. Then, after what seemed like an eternity, he turned to his 1SGs, "Do you have any questions?"

First Sergeant Dobbs from the Bravo Company asked me, "Corporal Arroyo, if you had to call for indirect fire using your compass, would you use mils or degrees?" That was a very easy question since I called many fire missions in Iraq and in training.

"I would use mils, First Sergeant."

Looking at the CSM, 1SG Dobbs said, "That's all I got, Sergeant Major."

"Anyone else have any questions?" All of the 1SGs shook their heads."

"Let me ask you a question," CSM Watts said as he leaned forward in his seat. "There are three types of dogs in this world." I maintained eye contact with him, but I could hear some of the 1SGs chuckling. CSM Watts continued in his classic black Southern style:

"There are three types of dogs. First you have a house dog. Now a house dawg, he in the house, eating good food, sleeping on a nice bed; and when a bad guy comes into the yard, he starts barking up a storm. But if you opened the door, the house dawg, he ain't gonna run out to the yard. No, the house dawg, he gonna run to his owner for protection.

"Then there's the porch dawg. The porch dawg, he stays on the porch, because he's too afraid to venture into the yard. When the bad guy comes along, the porch dawg turns to the house dawg and wants to climb in through the window."

Some of the 1SGs chuckled and I couldn't help but chuckle with them. CSM Watts smiled for a few seconds, then his serious face returned.

"Then you have a yard dawg. The yard dawg, he is the first line of defense. He is outside, rain, heat, or snow. He smells bad because he's always sleeping in the dirt or mud. While the house dawg and porch dawg eat the best food, hell, they be eatin' what the master be eatin'. But the yard dawg, he be eatin' dry kibble. He always angry, hoping the bad guy comes so he can bite 'em. While the house dawg and the porch dawgs be barking, the yard dawg, he don't bark. He just bite."

He watched me for a moment, then asked, "Which dawg are you?"

"I'm a yard dawg, Sergeant Major."

There was a pregnant pause after my response.

"Do you know the Ranger Creed?" Watts asked.

"Yes, Sergeant Major."

"Let me hear it."

I shot up out of my seat and I stood at attention. With a loud voice, I recited the Ranger Creed:

"Recognizing that I volunteered as a Ranger, fully knowing the hazards of my chosen profession, I will always endeavor to uphold the prestige, honor, and high esprit de corps of the Rangers!

"Acknowledging the fact that a Ranger is a more elite Soldier who arrives at the cutting edge of battle by land, sea, or air, I accept the fact that as a Ranger my country expects me to move further, faster and fight harder than any other Soldier!

"Never shall I fail my comrades. I will always keep myself mentally alert, physically strong and morally straight and I will shoulder more than my share of the task whatever it may be, one hundred percent and then some!

"Gallantly will I show the world that I am a specially selected and well-trained Soldier. My courtesy to superior officers, neatness of dress and care of equipment shall set the example for others to follow!

"Energetically will I meet the enemies of my country. I shall defeat them on the field of battle for I am better trained and will fight with all my might. Surrender is not a Ranger word. I will never leave a fallen comrade to fall into the hands of the enemy and under no circumstances will I ever embarrass my country!

"Readily will I display the intestinal fortitude required to fight on to the Ranger objective and complete the mission though I be the lone survivor!

"Rangers Lead the Way!"

"Woohoo!" CSM Watts was fired up. "I felt the walls shakin'!" he shouted. I stood at the position of attention wondering what I would have to do next.

"Alright, Sergeant. Congratulations. You're dismissed."

I saluted CSM Watts, and he stood and returned the salute. I turned and left the promotion board. I entered the room a corporal, and I left a sergeant.

CSM Watts really was a yard dawg. He parachuted from airplanes into combat, he was the lone survivor of a Blackhawk helicopter crash during a training exercise, he was a graduate of the Ranger School, and he took every opportunity to go out on combat missions with his paratroopers. On the night of 21 November 2006, CSM Watts went out on a mission with the men of Alpha Company, in the town of Saliah. As they were returning to base, just outside the gate 2 entrance of FOB Summerall, his Humvee drove over a double-stacked anti-tank mine.

CSM Watts was riding in the passenger seat and it was the front right tire which hit the landmine, killing him. The Humvee caught fire and the other passengers rushed to pull CSM Watts out. Through the flames

SSG Jason Dersch reached for Watts, but he was so severely burned his skin peeled off his arms. Dersch had to grab hold of his body armor to pull him out. Immediately paratroopers loaded him onto another Humvee and rushed him to the aid station. But CSM was already gone.

The call came over the radio for all personnel on the FOB to report to the aid station. We lined up in two single-file lines facing each other. The two lines extended from the front entrance of the aid station to the flight line. A Blackhawk medevac helicopter landed and the pilots shut off the propellers. Chaplain Kramer stood next to the Blackhawk door, with his Bible in hand.

"Battalion, attention!" We snapped to attention, and all five company 1SGs walked out of the aid station carrying a stretcher. On the stretcher was the body of CSM Watts, placed inside a black body bag, covered by the American flag. As the First Sergeants carried him to the medevac helicopter, we rendered our respects with one final salute. His body was loaded onto the Blackhawk and Chaplain Kramer said a prayer.

Later, a service was held for CSM Watts. We stood at parade rest and CSM Bryant "Debo" Lambert gave the eulogy. Lambert served over sixteen years in the Army with Watts, yet I was surprised when CSM Lambert paused during his eulogy because he could not hold back his tears any longer. After pausing for a few seconds, Lambert looked up at us and with a shaky voice said, "No one is invincible."

CSM Lambert then stood in front of the five company First Sergeants who were in a file formation facing the wooden box. CSM Watts's rifle was pointed down with his dog tags hanging from the buttstock, alongside his boots, and his photograph, wearing his maroon beret and a jovial smile.

"Battalion, attention!"

I was overwhelmed with sadness as the tears rolled down my face.

"First Sergeant Dobbs!"

"Here, Sergeant Major!"

"First Sergeant Green!"

"Here Sergeant Major!"

"Sergeant Major Watts!"

Through the silence I could hear sniffling as paratroopers were shedding tears.

"Command Sergeant Major Watts!"

Silence.

"Command Sergeant Major Donovan E. Watts!"

Silence.

"Present, arms!"

There was a muffled sound of commands as the honor guard sergeant gave orders to his paratroopers. "Detail, attention. Port, arms. Half right, face. Ready, aim, fire!" The three-round volleys echoed through the desert sky and each volley sent chills down my spine. The sound of three volleys was too familiar at this point, and it served to remind me another one of my brothers was dead. CSM Watts was the father figure for our battalion and the force keeping our unit working. After his passing away, our battalion was never the same.

SPC CHRISTOPHER E. MASON
KIA 28 November 2006, Bayji, Iraq

Our eight-hour graveyard guard duty shifts were brutal. It was hard for SPC Taylor and me to stay awake because there was no activity for us to observe. We were on guard duty in FOB Summerall and all we saw from 0000 hours to 0800 hours was darkness. Even the city lights went to sleep so we resorted to pounding energy drinks and sharing funny stories about our past or even recent combat missions. No topic was off limits on guard duty, so Taylor and I shared tales ranging from our sexual encounters with girls to embarrassing events of our past.

Then, that night—28 November 2006—there was an unexpected and unwelcome change to the monotony of our guard duty, and it began with a radio call from the Battalion Defense Operations Center.

"OP 3, this is BDOC, over."

"BDOC, this is OP 3, over," I responded.

"OP 3, OP 4, and OP 5, be advised that friendlies will be patrolling through your sector of fire . . . patrolling through Senea in four Humvees, over."

"BDOC, this is OP 3, that's a good copy, over."

"BDOC, out."

PFC Taylor and I began scanning our sector in search of the four Humvees. "I don't see a damn thing," Taylor said as he scanned the city of Senea using a thermal sight.

"I don't see them either. Maybe they haven't left the wire yet . . . Wait. I see 'em! They're driving east to west in front of OP 2, so they're coming our way."

"Yeah, I see them," responded Taylor. "I see their IR strobes."

The four trucks were driving slowly through the streets of Senea looking for worrisome activity. As they drove past our sector, the machine gunners in the turrets flashed their night vision IR strobe at us to make sure we were watching them. Taylor and I flashed our IR lights back as we provided overwatch from our guard tower, scanning the streets and rooftops. All was normal and there was no sign of suspicious activity. It was the usual boring night. Taylor and I were just glad we had something to look at.

We could still see the trucks as they turned left onto Market Street, where they were in OP 5's sector of fire. But suddenly my night vision was flooded by a bright light. *BOOM!* A ball of flames lit the night sky and gunfire erupted. Red tracer rounds from the machine gunners in the turrets flew down the streets of Senea and ricocheted off the concrete walls.

"BDOC, BDOC, this is OP 3, over!" I had to raise my voice over the gunfire.

"OP 3, this is BDOC, over."

"The Alpha Company element is in contact. They're being ambushed, over!"

"Roger that. We have QRF in route, over."

The flames grew larger, and the gunfire continued. Taylor and I scanned the city with our weapons, but we couldn't see anyone in the streets or rooftops. I switched our radio frequency to the battalion channel to listen in on A Co.'s situation.

"1 Panther 71, this is Alpha 16, over!" I could hear the background sound of machine guns fire through the hand mic of Alpha 16's radio transmission.

"Alpha 16, this is 1 Panther 71, over."

"We were ambushed on Market Street. We have one Humvee on fire and the driver is trapped inside, break . . . the truck was flipped upside down by the explosion and the doors won't open. The driver is trapped inside, over!"

Then the panicked voice of an NCO shouted, "Alpha 16, the doors won't open! Mason is inside and we can't get him out! We need the fire truck!"

"Break, break, break; Alpha 16, this is 1 Panther 71, QRF is in route with the fire truck and medics, use fire extinguishers and do whatever you can. They are in route, over."

A deep sense of hopelessness overwhelmed me as I heard those voices of rage and panic while watching fire flare up even higher. The insurgents placed a propane tank and two double-stacked anti-tank mines on the road. To increase the lethality of the IED, the insurgents also doused the street with gasoline. Market Street was on fire, a Humvee was flipped upside down, and a paratrooper was stuck inside and being burned alive. I listened to the radio and powerlessly watched as the events unfolded. There was nothing anyone could do to save Corporal Mason.

While the soldiers continued trying to rescue Mason, a fire team followed a trail of blood from an insurgent they wounded. The trail led them to a house down the street from the ambush. Upon entering, they found a man with an AK-47 next to him on the floor. He was an Iraqi soldier.

SPC Mason was a joy to be around. He was a lively character who always maintained a positive attitude. You always knew he was around because wherever he went, he made everyone laugh with his great sense of humor and his Southern twang. Back at Fort Bragg, I asked Mason, "Where you from in the States?"

"He smiled and said to me, in his Alabama accent, "I'm from LA, baby!""

"Wow," I said. "I'm from LA too. Where in LA are you from?"

He replied with a big smile, "Nah, I'm from Lower Alabama, baby!"

If you asked anyone in the 1-505 PIR about Mason, they would give you the response that every soldier from any elite unit works hard to achieve—and that response is "He's squared away."

SPC Christopher E. Mason really was squared away. He was God-fearing, a follower of Jesus Christ.

SGT. WILLIAM M. SIGUA
KIA 31 January 2007, Bayji, Iraq

It was a rare commodity to have the day off but, whenever I did, I spent it eating, sleeping, and working out. My friend SSG Szymczyk "Jerry" and I would sometimes work out twice a day, pushing each other's limits with a mix of high intensity interval training and weightlifting. One day, after a good workout, we headed to the chow hall for a hot meal. We grabbed our trays and went through the line, picking out whatever delicious food was being served. Then I scanned the hall for a good seat, preferably by one of the television sets. Just then I saw someone smiling and waving at me. It was SGT Will Sigua.

Sigua was a good friend of mine and I wasn't able to talk to him during our deployment because we were in different companies. I sat with him and enjoyed our meal together. I remember laughing hard a couple of times to the point of almost spitting out my food. Sigua was making fun of all the stupid NCOs in Charlie Company.

Later on, Sigua sparked up a cigarette and we talked for a few more minutes. After more funny stories and good laughs, it was time for us to part ways and return to our respective company areas. "Alright, brother," I said, "I love you. Stay safe."

"I love you too. Stay safe and I'll see you around," We hugged and parted ways.

The next day, on 31 January 2007, after returning from a patrol, we received a call on the radio from the battalion headquarters. "Guidons,

guidons, guidons, this is 1 Panther 71. All troops report to the battalion aid station, over."

Something was wrong, and we all knew what it was. Someone died. There was no other reason for such a call over the radio, except to gather to pay our final respects to a fallen paratrooper. We quickly gathered our platoon and walked over to the aid station. Slowly, men trickled in to gather in front of the aid station. "Anyone know what's happening?" I heard the question more than once, but we all knew the answer.

Then a paratrooper said the words no one wanted to hear: "Someone died."

"Do you know who?" I asked, hoping it was not one of my close friends.

"I'm not sure, I heard his battle roster over the radio. His last name starts with the letter 'S'."

"S? What company was he with?"

"Charlie Company," he answered.

Who do I know with a last name that begins with the letter S? I asked myself. The first name that came to mind was Sully. *No, not Sully!* I thought. He and I have been to hell and back together since our time in Fallujah.

There was only one other name that came to mind, and it was Sigua.

Just then I heard, "Line up! Two lines facing each other. All the way down to the flight line." I heard the propellers of an incoming helicopter.

Not again, I thought.

We lined up and the helicopter landed on the flight line. The pilot shut off the engines, and Chaplain Kramer emerged from the aid station with tears rolling down his cheeks, with his Bible in his left hand. He didn't look up. He just walked with his head down toward the helicopter and he stood next to the door.

First Sergeant Green called the battalion to attention and the plywood door of the aid station opened. From out of the aid station emerged Sully, SGT Rubio, SGT Alzate, and three others, carrying a green stretcher with a black body bag on top of it, covered by the American flag. It was SGT William M. Sigua.

As they walked toward the Blackhawk, we rendered our final salute. I didn't cry, instead I was filled with rage. *Who did this?* I wanted revenge. It was believed to be the same sniper who shot RV.

It happened while C Co. 2nd Platoon was in the city of Bayji; 2nd Platoon was tasked with providing security near the Bayji traffic circle. They were to remain there for twenty-four hours, so the men had to take turns manning the machine gun in the turret to allow for bathroom breaks, food, sleep, and water.

As a squad leader, Sigua did not have to man the Humvee turret. But he was not the type of leader who would watch his men do all the work. Wanting his soldiers to get rest, Sigua volunteered to man the turret and protect his soldiers so they could rest.

Early in the morning, as the sun was rising, a single shot was fired. One of the paratroopers looked toward the turret of the Humvee to ask SGT Sigua if he knew where the shot came from. Instead, he saw Sigua slouched on the turret with his head down.

"He's hit! SGT Sigua's hit!" But by that time Sigua's pulse was fading fast, and he wasn't breathing.

The call came over the radio and SGT Sullivan and the medic rushed to Sigua's aid. It was too late and there was nothing anyone could do. Sigua was hit in the back of his head, at the base of his skull.

"He's f------ dead!" yelled Sully. "Quit standing around and let's go!" The paratroopers went into the building where they thought the shot came from, then maneuvered through several other buildings with the hope of finding the sniper. He was gone, and so was Sigua.

~ ~ ~

I remembered the best Thanksgiving I'd ever had was in North Carolina in 2005. Our Battalion didn't get leave for Thanksgiving Day, so Sully decided we would celebrate Thanksgiving at his house. My buddies called their moms and asked for their favorite recipes. Once we got the ingredients and the instructions, we went to the grocery store and bought everything we needed—especially alcohol. Since it was Sully's house and he wanted Thanksgiving to be "classy," we were told only to buy wine, and we purchased more than enough. I don't remember how many boxes, cases, or bottles there were, but we had enough wine to kill a healthy whale.

My buddy Knouse made cheesy potatoes, SGT Bougere a.k.a. Bugger made deviled eggs, and I helped Sully with the turkey. Alzate, Rubio, CPL Palmer, SPC Toups, RV, SGT Pena, SGT Harmon, and Sigua were there and made their home recipes. The entire process of cooking was done while consuming vast amounts of wine. We didn't have wine glasses, so we drank straight from the bottle.

We set up a couple of foldable tables and chairs in the backyard and we draped both tables with a white tablecloth. By the time the food was ready, we were all pretty wasted. After setting the table, we brought out the food and served it. It was mandatory for each paratrooper to have two bottles of wine with him at the table. Once seated, because it was Sully's house, and we were wasted, Sully wanted us to say what we were thankful for. Sully sat at the head of the table, and he was the first to share what he was thankful for.

"I'm thankful to still be alive, even though I thought I would have died a warrior in battle, taking as many *hadjis* as I could with me. I'm thankful for you f------s! There's no other group of ass-----s I would rather spend this day with!"

"I love you too, Sully," said Toups, slurring his words.

We went around the table, sharing how there was nowhere else we would rather be for Thanksgiving, and we devoured the food in front of us. By the end of the night, some of us got sick and passed out. We couldn't spend our Thanksgiving with our families back home, so we spent it together, as brothers.

SGT Will Sigua was my brother.

CPL Eric C. Palmer
KIA 24 June 2007, Bayji, Iraq

It was another day of FOB security and I was the NCOIC (non-commissioned officer in charge) at gate 1. It was a bad start to an eight-hour shift duty at gate 1 when a call came over the battalion radio.

"We have one friendly wounded, break . . ." the familiar tone of sadness and anger continued, "He is urgent surgical. The medevac helicopter is in route, over."

I felt chills go down my spine. *Please, don't be someone I know*, I thought.

"Bayji CP, this is 1 Panther 71, I copy all. What is the soldier's battle roster number, over?"

Bayji CP meant it was Charlie Company, so I listened intently for the letter of the battle roster number which is the first letter of the soldier's last name and the last four digits of his social security number. I don't remember the number, but the first letter was "P."

No way! Was it Pena? Was it Palmer? I grabbed my Icom radio and called Weise back at the BDOC.

"Bravo 14, this is Bravo 11, over."

"Bravo 11, this is Bravo 14, over."

"Do you know the name of the guy who was hit, over."

"Yeah—his name's Palmer, over."

"Roger."

"Damnit! No f------ way!" I screamed inside the guard shack. Another one of my friends was killed. *Why were all the good guys dying? Why couldn't it have been someone I didn't like?* I said out loud to myself. Palmer was a great paratrooper. He saved me from a tight spot back at Bragg.

One night back in Fayetteville, I was out drinking at a bar with Knouse and some of our friends from C Co., when the bouncers came over to our table and kicked us out. Apparently, we were too drunk and some of my friends were harassing women and trying to start fights with patrons. A few of them had to be thrown out.

Once we were outside the bar, two drunk guys started pushing some of my friends around. When the fight broke out, we all joined in, mostly to save our buddies from getting hurt. Outnumbered, one of the two drunk guys pulled out his gun and shot it into the air. My buddies fled the scene immediately, but I didn't. After shooting his pistol, the man pointed it at me.

"Run and I'll kill you!" he yelled at me. I stood there with my hands up, looking him in the eye. With a calm voice I said to him, "Put the gun down. You don't want to shoot me. You'll go to jail for life, and I'm not worth it."

"Shut the hell up!" he yelled back at me, with his finger on the trigger. The only thing between him and me was a blue sedan.

One of the two drunk guys feeling brave decided to try and punch RV but Knouse intervened and knocked him down. We made easy work of the two, but now I was alone, with my bloodied hands up, listening to the gunman's beat-up friend groaning on the ground.

And now the police were on their way. I could hear their sirens getting closer and I knew I could go to jail for this.

Just then I heard a voice: "Why are you still here?"

It was Knouse. He ran off thinking I was with him. But when he noticed I wasn't there, he came back to get me.

"Dude!" I said surprised. "Now we're both gonna get shot."

Knouse looked at the man with the gun, "He ain't doing nothin', let's get out of here."

"If you try to leave, I'll kill the both of you!" shouted the gunman.

"You ain't gonna do nothin'!" Knouse shouted back. "Let's go!"

The sirens were closer, and I trusted Knouse with my life, so I decided to run with him.

"If you shoot me while I'm running away, you're going to jail for life."

"If you run, I'll kill you!" the drunk man shouted, holding what looked to be a chrome 9mm pistol in his right hand.

"Later, dude!"

I heard the drunk yelling behind us as we sprinted away. Knouse and I ran on the road until we heard sirens and saw red and blue lights through the trees. I counted four police cars speeding toward the scene, followed by an ambulance, and then two more police cars behind the ambulance.

We headed for the trees.

"We need to set up a rendezvous," I told Knouse as we ran.

"Sully's on CQ. I'll call him to send someone." Knouse pulled out his phone and called the Charlie Company CQ (charge of quarter) desk.

PFC Palmer answered.

"Palmer, this is Knouse. Where is Sully?"

"I think he's drinking upstairs, what's up?"

"Tell him we need help."

"All right. Stand by."

We kept moving through the woods. By then we were in a shallow swamp, about ankle deep in mud.

Finally, Sully came on the line. "Sully, this is Knouse. I think we might have killed a guy and now the police are after us. We need a ride out of here."

"Who's with you?"

"Arroyo's with me."

"Where are you?"

"We're walking in the woods toward a gas station."

"Give me the cross streets and I'll send Palmer to get you guys."

Using the cover of darkness and the trees, Knouse and I moved toward the back of the gas station. We took a knee in the woods and watched the gas station for a few seconds to check for any law enforcement activity. No one was around, so I walked close enough to see the names of the cross streets.

"We're behind a gas station on the corner of Joe and Jane Streets," I whispered into the phone and then returned to the wood line with Knouse.

"Alright, I see it on the map. Palmer will be there in ten minutes. He is in a faded red Chevy Blazer. He's going to park facing east, toward the gas station, and he will flash his headlights twice. Got it?"

"Got it."

"Alright. Call me if anything changes."

"Okay. Later."

Ten minutes seems like an eternity when you're being pursued by the police. Knouse and I were sitting in the woods, staring at the gas station, when we spotted a patrol car driving west toward the intersection.

"Stay low," I whispered.

The officer turned left at the intersection where he could see the back of the gas station. Knouse and I laid down and covered ourselves with brush. We stayed flat to the ground and kept our ankles flat as possible. I saw the officer looking at the gas station and then behind it. I saw his eyes focusing in on the wood line and he looked right in our direction. I thought his eyes squinted.

Damn, he saw us, I thought. My heart was pounding in my chest as the officer grabbed his hand mic and started talking to dispatch, but he kept driving.

"Holy crap, man," Knouse whispered to me. "Where's Palmer?"

Just then we saw an SUV park at the corner. "Is that him?" I asked Knouse. The SUV shut off its headlights. We watched intently, hoping that it was Palmer. Then the headlights flashed twice, and we knew we were finally closer to getting home.

We took a quick look around and there were no vehicles on the road and no sign of the police. "Let's go, dude," I whispered to Knouse. We looked both ways and emerged from the woods covered in swamp mud and leaves. We jogged past a blonde woman who was starting to pump gas.

"Oh my God!" she cried, startled by the two of us emerging from the wilderness covered in mud. She probably thought we were dangerous. I smiled and waved at the two elementary-aged kids in the back seat and kept moving toward Palmer and the SUV.

"Hey!" Palmer was wearing BDUs and a big smile. "You guys look like s---, and you smell like it too! Haha!"

~ ~ ~

On June 24, 2007, our friend Palmer was shot by a sniper during a patrol in the city of Bayji. He was in the rear of the patrol, watching his brothers' backs. As they made their way toward the Bayji JSS (joint security station), Palmer turned to look behind him and he was shot on his right cheek. He was knocked onto his back. His squad opened fire in the direction of the incoming round and threw smoke grenades to cover their movement. They carried Palmer to cover, and the medic began to provide him with aid. A medevac helicopter was in the air within seconds.

Palmer was evacuated to COB Speicher, but his heart stopped upon arrival. He was resuscitated and moved to a hospital in Germany. His heart stopped once again when he arrived. Finally, Palmer reached the States, but the doctors told his parents the only thing keeping his heart beating was the life support machines. Palmer had no brain wave activity and was in a vegetative state. Palmer's parents had to make the difficult decision to disconnect their beloved son from the life support machines. His body was dead, but his soul was with the Lord.

Chapter Thirty-Two

Almost Burned

MANY OF MY brothers lost their lives, but our missions never stopped. One beautiful Iraqi morning, our platoon headed to the Bayji Oil Refinery (BOR). Our mission was to make ID cards for every BOR employee, to help us identify anyone who was not supposed to be in the refinery. This, we hoped, would also help us identify the al-Qaeda in Iraq terrorists and others, who were sneaking into the refinery to steal fuel to sell in Syria and Jordan for three times what it cost in Iraq. The BOR was a source of funding for terrorists, Iranians, and the Chinese, all of whom were in on it.

I was in the lead Humvee when we pulled up to the building where we intended to start making ID cards. I saw a white sedan parked in front of the building, so I called in a possible vehicle improvised explosive device (VBIED). I told my driver, SPC Carlson a.k.a. Noslrac (we butchered his name) to stop the truck and I dismounted to investigate the car. As I approached, a man came out from the building, and in broken English, he asked me if I wanted him to move his vehicle. I looked inside the car, including the trunk, and it was clear, so I told him to move it.

While the man started the engine and slowly moved his vehicle, Weise, Jerry, and, Rademacher left their trucks and were standing next to me. Once the car moved, Jerry ordered his driver, Anthony Kittrell, to move the truck to the right side of the building. Toups and the machine gunner, Kittrell, made their way to the side of the building to provide security for us, while we made ID cards.

Then *BOOM!* The blast wave shook my body and broke several windows in the nearby buildings. Clumps of dirt and mud rained on us, hitting my helmet and body armor.

As Toups drove the truck to the side of the building, he ran over a double-stacked anti-tank mine, stacked above an underground propane tank. I took a knee and heard gunfire behind me. When I turned around, I saw Weise shooting at the windows of a building where he saw a possible triggerman, so I joined in and fired thirty rounds, destroying every window of a one-story office building. Then I heard machine gun fire and watched as other troopers shot their .50-caliber and M-240B machine guns at vehicles fleeing the scene.

"Ceasefire! Ceasefire! Ceasefire!" I yelled at the top of my lungs. When the shooting stopped, I ran to the upside-down Humvee on the side of the building. The truck was on fire.

SPC Miller ran out to meet me.

"Are they still in there?" I urgently asked him.

"I think they're still inside!"

"Damn! Bring me some fire extinguishers!" I ordered Miller.

As Miller ran to his Humvee to get the extinguishers, I yelled, "Kittrell! Toups! Are you in there!" I shouted repeatedly for Kittrell and Toups, but there was no response. Miller handed me a fire extinguisher and we began to spray the flames.

My fire extinguisher was soon empty, and the flames were still rising. I called for Kittrell and Toups several times, but there was no response.

I have to save them, I said to myself, as I stood feet away from the burning Humvee and felt the extreme heat. *I have to save them!*

I made up my mind to run through the flames, open the rear Humvee door and pull Kittrell and Toups out, before they burned alive. "Three," I started a countdown in my head. "Two," as I slightly bent my knees so I could sprint through the flames. "One," I was about to sprint forward when I heard, "Sergeant Arroyo! We're over here!"

I lurched to a stop, looked to my left, and saw Toups and Kittrell beside some bushes, just fifteen feet from the truck, sitting on the ground. They looked beat up, with red and bruised faces, and bloody noses.

When the truck exploded and turned on its side, Toups was blown from the driver seat. When he came to, he made his way to Kittrell, who was unconscious and trapped in the Humvee's turret. Toups used his knife to cut a strap holding Kittrell and managed to pull him out of the turret. He dragged him away from the burning Humvee and into the bushes for cover and concealment.

Of course, I was happy to see them alive, but for a moment I also felt like an idiot. I thought about how stupid it would have been had I run through the flames and into the burning vehicle only to find no one inside. Nonetheless, I was happy to have felt the passion that drove me toward them. The bond between us as warriors was indescribably powerful. That Toups would risk his life to save his brother was caused by a bond few people ever experience.

When we were back at FOB Summerall, Rademacher (Rod) and I talked about what happened earlier that day. Rod was an atheist for some time. One day he and I had a conversation about the Bible and Rod told me the Bible was all lies, and science could explain everything from a naturalistic approach. I wasn't a good Christian, but deep down in my heart, I knew God was real. I mostly struggled with whether I wanted to pray to Him or obey Him. But I challenged Rod to read the Bible, and he did. He read the entire Bible.

Rod told me when I called in the possible VBIED at the refinery, he felt something was wrong, so he prayed to Jesus Christ. When Jerry dismounted the Humvee, Rod felt compelled to join him. The damage assessment of the Humvee later proved it was the rear left tire of the Humvee that detonated the IED. Rod was sitting in the rear left seat and, had he not exited the truck, he would have died. Rod had a somewhat confused look on his face as he shared this experience with me.

He wondered if he experienced a miracle from God, or if it was all just a coincidence.

Chapter Thirty-Three

Mayhem

ON JUNE 25, 2007, my platoon and I were on our way to FOB Summerall after three days of living in the oil refinery and carrying out operations to disrupt insurgent activity near and around the city of Bayji, Iraq. As we drove back to the FOB, my fellow squad leader, Jerry, noticed a tire sitting on the side of the road. It looked like a wire was sticking out from under it. He quickly reported this to our lieutenant. We then proceeded to stop traffic on both sides of Highway Tampa, which runs north to south. Our lieutenant contacted battalion headquarters (1 Panther 71) to inform them of our situation and awaited the explosive ordnance disposal (EOD) unit. It usually took an hour for EOD to arrive at any location.

While our platoon waited inside our Humvees for them to arrive, Jerry (Bravo One Two) called me (Bravo One One) over the radio and told me to exit my Humvee and to look toward the city of Bayji, which was located some five miles north of our position. There I saw a huge mushroom cloud rising from within the city and recognized by the size of the cloud, it had to have been a vehicle-born improvised explosive device (VBIED).

I quickly got back into my Humvee and changed the radio frequency to battalion to hear what was happening. Over the radio I could hear one of my friends, who I served with in Iraq and Afghanistan, say "Bayji VBIED," but his voice was very weak. It sounded like he was gasping for air.

Battalion headquarters quickly responded to this call for help but there was no answer from Charlie Company's net. C Co. was responsible for conducting combat operations in the city of Bayji from a joint security station (JSS) adjacent to an Iraqi police station. After several attempts at contacting C Co., our lieutenant radioed to inform battalion headquarters that based on recent events, C Co. was likely attacked by a suicide VBIED and needed help. At that point battalion headquarters ordered our platoon to return to the Bayji Oil Refinery and wait for further instructions.

Once we arrived at the refinery our platoon leader (PL) informed us C Co. had, in fact, been hit by a VBIED and they were being overrun by approximately twenty or more insurgents. It was a planned and coordinated attack by the enemy who, of course, wanted to kill every coalition troop in the JSS. Our job would be to repel the attack and drive the attackers away from the JSS so our wounded troops could be evacuated, and control of the city would be restored.

This was unreal. I felt my heart racing as I heard what was taking place and knew my friends from C Co. were dead, wounded, or about to be. I was in charge of the lead Humvee and was ordered to drive to the front of the JSS in order to create a barrier between C Co. and the insurgents. We were on a rescue mission headed straight into gunfire and chaos.

As we drove to the JSS, SGT "Marty" Holland said a prayer. "Dear Lord, I ask that you protect the men of Charlie Company and protect us as we enter this chaos. In the name of our Lord, Jesus Christ, Amen." I heard Noslrac and Taylor, who claimed to be atheists, say, "Yes Jesus, protect us." This made Marty angry because Taylor and Noslrac would persistently make fun of Marty's faith.

"Don't make fun of Jesus! It's not funny!" Marty shouted.

"No, Marty." Noslrac and Taylor said. "Keep praying." I guess there really are no atheist in foxholes.

I said a prayer in my mind and realized I had not gone to church in a couple of years. I was harboring anger toward God for being stop loss, for Sarah leaving me, and for my friends dying. I blamed God for all of my suffering and, even though I thought about Him, I stopped myself from praying to Him. That day, in that moment, as we drove toward the mushroom cloud and to what could possibly be my last combat mission, I prayed.

"Lord, forgive me for my sins. If I die, may I awake in your presence. Amen."

After a few minutes of driving north on highway Tampa, we arrived at the JSS and began taking sniper fire. I told my gunner (Taylor) to stay low in the turret and return fire only if he identified a shooter.

As we approached the JSS it looked like a Hollywood set designed to portray a nuclear attack site. There was a huge crater on the street directly in front of the JSS where the suicide bomber drove into a concrete barrier meant to protect what used to be an Iraqi police station. The streets were riddled with car parts and rubble. I noticed a white Nissan pickup truck wrapped around the middle section of a telephone pole. Fear gripped me as I prepared to leave the Humvee to check on C Co.—the fear of the unknown. I had many concerns prior to arriving at the JSS. I wondered if Sullivan was dead and began to brace myself in case I saw his dead body in the debris or the corpse of any other American.

I got out of my truck and walked to the rubble. I stood over the rubble and saw the mangled bodies of several Iraqi policemen. I was fixated on one corpse. I was standing over his body; he was pale blue and partially covered with gray concrete dust from the shattered walls. He had no face, and where he should have had a nose, eyes, ears, and mouth, there was nothing left. A hole providing me with a clear view of what brain matter he had left inside his skull now occupied the space where his face had been. Next to him in the rubble to my right was another Iraqi policeman, also covered in concrete dust and several large pieces of rubble. His face was intact, but his torso contained several baseball-size holes from shrapnel ripping through his body.

A white ambulance with a red crescent moon on the rear window suddenly appeared to my right. The paramedics backed in close to where more bodies were hidden under the rubble. I watched as two men wearing white collared shirts and black pants rapidly got out and opened the rear double doors of the ambulance. I watched as they removed the Iraqi with the holes in his torso. They picked him up, with one paramedic lifting his legs and the other placing his hands under his armpits. They carried him gently into the back of the ambulance and softly lowered his body. They both quickly jumped out, closed the doors, and ran to the ambulance cab. They turned on the red lights and sirens and drove off.

I watched the ambulance disappear behind tall concrete barrier walls as the paramedics turned left. The sound of the sirens slowly faded away and an eerie silence once again flooded the atmosphere. I turned my attention back to the bodies in the rubble when I heard footsteps. I saw Sullivan approaching me. He was wearing his boots, ACU bottoms, tan T-shirt, body armor, and helmet. Blood oozed from his nose, and his eyes were watery. I stepped across some rubble to get to him and asked if he was all right. "My guys and I killed over twenty insurgents."

At that moment I felt a sense of relief to know Sullivan was fine and he was ready to kick ass. He told me to watch for enemy fire from a building located southwest of the JSS. The three-story building was on the corner of Highway One and RPG alley He also told me the insurgents booby trapped the road between the JSS and F.O.B. Summerall with twenty or more IED's, so QRF would not get to us for another hour or so. He also told me there were no available air assets because they were providing close air support to other troops, or on their way to refuel and rearm. "We're gonna be on our own for at least an hour, so tell your guys to conserve ammo."

After Sullivan explained the situation to me, I informed the rest of my platoon. Then Young, Horan, SGT Holland, and I made our way through what used to be an Iraqi police station to check for living Iraqi police officers. We quickly learned there weren't any.

Lying on the ground amid the destruction were the corpses of several Iraqi policemen missing limbs. One in particular caught my attention because he had no face. I blocked all emotions, by instinct, and began to make my way toward the casualty collection point of the JSS.

There I saw wounded Iraqi soldiers and I watched as the medics tried to stop the hemorrhaging from the huge baseball-size holes on their backs created by shrapnel. I asked the medics if they needed any help. They said they had everything under control.

We started to head back to our trucks when we began taking fire, and it was coming from multiple directions. From the third floor of the building to the southwest, insurgents were firing AK-47s. I engaged the third-floor threats. Meanwhile C Co. troopers located on the roof of the JSS engaged the third floor of the building and other enemy combatants approaching the JSS from the north. The insurgents used a garbage truck, moving at about five to ten miles per hour, as cover to get close enough to enter our perimeter. From the roof top, C Co, fired MK-19 40mm grenade rounds and .50-caliber machine guns at the garbage truck. The enemy was decimated.

The back-and-forth shooting was intense, and it lasted about an hour. The insurgents were maneuvering on our position in groups of five to ten, from different directions. As we shot several insurgents in the third-floor building, I felt a sharp pain on my right ear, followed by a loud ring. Marty fired his weapon next to my right ear and the stinging pain was unbearable.

While I stuck my index finger in my ear, hoping it would bring some sort of comfort, Weise ordered troopers SGT Row and SPC Helgesen to fire AT-4 rockets at the building's third floor. When those rockets hit, all the paratroopers on the roof top of the JSS and on the street in front broke out in cheers and applause to taunt the insurgents. Not long after the AT-4 explosions, a Kiowa helicopter air weapons team and two AH-64 Apache helicopters arrived and began shooting targets designated by our forward observers.

I believe we all felt the same. Every paratrooper there was angry, frustrated, and eager to destroy all of Iraq. What this VBIED really did was give us an excuse to carry out our innermost violent ambitions toward the enemy. Insurgents came out from behind walls and shot bursts of fire at us before hiding again. Troopers Ayala, Toups, and SGT Winner killed them with their .50-cal. and M-240 machine guns.

I often felt like a spectator when it seemed like everything around me was happening in slow motion. I watched as the tracer rounds, glowing bright red, flew into their targets. I watched Cadena shoot a 40mm grenade into the third-story window of the southwest building and saw the round fly, enter the room, and explode. One second after that 40mm round exploded, a Kiowa helicopter fired two rockets into the same floor. I watched transfixed as sparks and concrete fell from the sky.

I was out on the street, using the rear of my Humvee as cover, and shooting at insurgents as they peeked out to take shots at us. I felt another sting, this time in my left ear. "F--- Marty! Check your fire!" Marty fired close to my left ear this time, and now both of my ears were hurting. The pain was severe, and I feared permanent damage and hearing loss. It would be a whole week before my hearing would return to normal.

At one point during the firefight, the Kiowa helicopters ran out of ammunition, so the pilots and copilots began shooting M-4s from their side doors and even throwing hand grenades on an insurgent casualty collection point. There were about thirty wounded insurgents gathered in a courtyard, receiving medical aid. The Kiowa crews dropped hand grenades on the insurgents and then marked the casualty point with a red smoke grenade. The forward observers used the smoke to coordinate 120mm mortar fire. They annihilated every one of the insurgents.

Before long, a F-16 arrived at the scene and made several low flying passes while dropping flares to frighten the enemy. But by then, the fight was over, and the enemy failed to take the JSS. As the F-16 made its passes, Cadena picked up a human foot from the street. The foot was detached from the ankle and probably belonged to one of the Iraqi policemen. I laughed as Cadena walked over to a Humvee where Horan was sitting in the back seat, enjoying a cold bottle of water. Cadena opened the door and tossed the foot at Horan, hitting him in the face.

By then the QRF was en route to our location with replacement concrete barriers. We had to move our Humvees off the street and into the JSS. I walked over to where we were going to park the truck and called Noslrac over.

"What's up?"

"I need you to move our Humvee and park it in here. Put it closer to the left."

"Alright."

Boom! I heard a loud pop and saw dirt splash in front of me, just inches from my feet.

"What the hell was that?" I asked Noslrac.

He laughed out loud. "I think someone's trying to kill you, Sergeant." I sprinted forward, grabbing Noslrac and moved us to cover behind a concrete wall. Jerry saw what happened. "Holy crap, man. You got lucky. That sniper almost got you." I wondered if the sniper who shot at me was the same Chechen sniper scoring head shots on my friends.

"Noslrac, go get the Humvee."

Once I was behind cover, I paused for a moment looking at the mangled bodies and the giant crater in the street. I stared at the white pickup truck wrapped around a telephone poll and thought about the sniper who missed me by just a few inches.

Yes, someone was looking after me. A higher power was with me, and I could feel His presence. I knew who He was but I still hated Him. I had made my mind up to go into a dark place. I heard reports we killed over 170 people that day—all in that one hour—and I could only smile.

Chapter Thirty-Four

Snake Eaters

DESPITE OUR LOSSES, our missions continued. We had a war to win. I had to ignore my emotions, burying them deep inside, and focus on the work ahead. Before long, we were on a mission to kill or capture high value targets.

We entered the small town of Henshi, on the outskirts of Bayji, Iraq, riding in four Humvees. The streets looked green through my night vision as we quietly left our vehicles and made our way to the target house—the home of an IED maker and his cousin who were in business with al-Qaeda in Iraq and the Iranians. These bad guys were responsible for creating the bombs that killed or wounded several American and allied troops in our area over the years, and now they were going to pay the price.

The house was surrounded by a six-foot wall. Weise and Cadena moved toward the front gate to enter, but it was locked. There was a mound of sand on our side of the wall so, instead of breaching the door, I used the mound to climb over as Weise, Cadena, Jerry, and Horan covered the front door and windows of the house. I could see their infrared lasers as I climbed over the wall and made my way to the gate. I disabled the latch keeping the gate locked and let the rest of our guys inside. We stacked in front of the house, just to the left of the front door, and signaled for the breacher, Dusty Noslrac, and he moved up to check the door.

He gently turned the doorknob and nodded at me to let me know it was unlocked. Almost every house I entered in Iraq had an unlocked door, which made our entries a surprise. Noslrac and I quietly and quickly entered the living room, making sure to clear the corners. We flowed through the house and silently cleared each room. We trained exhaustively, back at Fort Bragg, on how to enter and clear buildings and rooms, so we didn't have to say a word. We just used our head nods and hand signals as we made our way through the house. In the typical Iraqi home, there was usually a room where the women and children slept. In the summertime, the men slept on the roof to get out of the heat of the concrete home.

I made my way into a room where I saw the women and children sleeping, with the exception of one older female. She was holding a baby, no more than a couple of months old. She almost screamed as she gasped when she saw me enter the room in full kit, but she placed her right hand over her mouth to keep herself quiet, while still holding the baby with her left arm.

Noslrac and I quickly scanned the room and then left Hanson to watch the women and children, while the rest of us moved to the rooftop. I was point man so I headed up the stairs first, followed by Noslrac, Cadena, Weise, Horan, and SGT Rowe. The door at the end of the stairway was open so we streamed onto the rooftop. I saw three men sleeping on the thinly padded mats commonly used in Iraq. I walked up to the three men and quickly identified two of them as being the HVTs (high value targets).

I watched one of the terrorists sleeping and thought, *Wow, this is the scumbag making IEDs*. I pulled out a pair of zip tie handcuffs and gently grabbed the guy's hand, sliding his left wrist into the zip tie loop and then tightening it. Then, less gently, I rolled him over onto his stomach and placed his right wrist into the zip tie, tightening it nice and firmly. As I tightened the zip tie, he stopped snoring.

He woke up and panicked when he couldn't move his arms. I rolled him over and his eyes were wide open, trying to figure out what he was looking at. I wore my ACUs, IBA, Oakley clear lens eye protection, ACH with infrared strobe lights attached and PVS-14 night vision, my M-4 with Surefire tactical flashlight with IR cap, PEQ-2 infrared laser, hand grenades, flash-bangs, mag pouches, and Oakley carbon fiber knuckle gloves. He looked around and saw more guys just like me, wearing the same gear. His eyes opened even wider, and his jaw dropped in shock and dread when he realized who we were.

~ ~ ~

This was Operation Snake Eater, and we were hunting the bad guys terrorizing the city of Bayji and the surrounding areas. As part of that operation, we went out on counter IED missions. The 2nd squad, led by Jerry, and the weapons squad, led by Weise, left the Bayji Oil Refinery to overwatch a road where insurgents were placing a high volume of IEDs. My 1st squad, and 3rd squad, led by SSG Young, stayed back at the BOR JSS to provide security. Before 2nd squad and weapons squad left the wire, I was joking around with Mack Miller and Daniel Garrard.

"Where ya' going?" I asked them.

"To end 'the corruption.' Someone's gotta do it, and we're it," said Miller. By "the corruption," he was referring to the massive theft of petroleum from the Bayji Oil Refinery.

"Damn! That's some hardcore airborne ops you're getting yourself into."

"Yeah, but we're ninjas so we got this," SPC Garrard said laughing.

It was time for them to leave the wire and everyone was loaded into the four Humvees and heading out. I looked at Weise and told him,

"I love you. Stay safe."

"Man, I be staying safe, homie!" Weise shouted.

I told Miller and Garrard the same thing. "I love you. Stay safe."

"I love you too," they both said.

As they drove off into the night, Jerry looked at me through the passenger side bulletproof window and blew me a kiss.

About an hour later I was getting into bed, after checking that everyone on guard duty was alert and doing their job. I laid down to rest when I heard Jerry's voice over the radio.

"BOR CP, this is Bravo One Two, over!"

"Bravo One Two, this is BOR CP, over."

"Bravo 14 just got hit by an IED, we have two wounded. They are urgent surgical and we're engaging the IED triggermen, over!"

I could hear another sergeant's voice on the battalion net radio, he was calling the 9-line medevac.

"Get your gear on!" I shouted to my troopers. We quickly got loaded on the Humvees and made our way to Weise and Jerry as fast as we could. Before we reached their location, the medics were already rushing to get to the Bayji Oil Refinery from where the two wounded men would be evacuated. We moved our Humvees to the side of the road and out of the way so they could keep going. Once they passed us, we made a U-turn and headed back to the aid station. When we got there I jumped out of my Humvee and ran inside. Doc McClean and Doc Pakaizer were finishing up bandaging Miller and Garrard.

Miller was driving the Humvee with Garrard sitting behind him when the IED exploded under the driver seat. Miller lost his left triceps and left calf muscle. Garrard had a piece of shrapnel tear through his left foot, and he was knocked unconscious, along with everyone else in the Humvee.

When Weise, who was sitting in the passenger seat, came to, he reached over the radios in the center console and grabbed the steering wheel as the Humvee rolled to a stop, with Miller's forehead on the steering wheel. When the truck stopped, Ayala (a.k.a. The Rooster, a.k.a. Silverback) fired the M-240B machine gun at a vehicle driving off at about 250 meters away. Weise then helped Doc McClean pull Miller and Garrard out of the Humvee so he could provide aid.

Now I was in the aid station wrapping a woobie around Garrard because he was in shock. "It's so cold," Garrard told me as I wrapped him with the blanket. His eyes were glossy, and his skin was a pale blue. I gently rubbed his shoulders to create some heat, when I heard the medevac helicopter propellers chopping the wind.

"Let's go, head for the LZ! Bad Blood 5 is inbound!" shouted Doc Pakaizer.

I helped Doc McClean carry Garrard on the stretcher while Weise and others helped carry Miller. Doc Pak marked the LZ with chem lights using a "NATO T" to let the pilot know where to land. The helicopter descended next to us on the LZ, and the propellers pushed dirt and cold wind on us, so I covered Garrard by gently placing my upper body and arms around his head to protect him from the debris.

"I'm sorry, dad! I'm sorry! I don't want to leave you!" Miller told Weise.

"It's okay, boo! I love you too!" Weise said.

I told Garrard, "You're gonna be okay!" Garrard looked pale blue and was shaking as he told me, "I love you! I don't want to go!" Even facing death, these warriors were more concerned about leaving their brothers behind. The helicopter medic exited the bird and Doc Pak approached him. Then the helicopter medic shouted, "What do we got?!"

"Two urgent surgical! This one lost his left calf and left triceps, and he's lost a lot of blood! This one has a hole in his left foot, and he lost a lot of blood as well!" Doc Pak shouted to the crew chief, over the sound of the rotors.

We loaded Miller and Garrard on the bird and the crew chief yelled, "Get back! Get back!" as he hopped back into the helicopter and they flew off. There was an eerie silence after the helicopter left the BOR. I watched Doc McClean place his hands on his head as he walked away from the rest of us with tears rolling down his cheeks. He just saved two of our brothers and he was coming down from the adrenaline rush.

It was 0500 and the sun was rising. My team and I loaded into four Humvees and visited the area of the attack. The crater left from the IED blast was about three feet in diameter. I found a copper wire used to detonate the bomb. Rowe and I followed it for two hundred meters to a trench where we located an empty sandbag and a 6-volt industrial battery used to detonate the bomb.

The reality of my situation set in. I was hunting human beings and they were hunting me. My heart filled with rage as I wanted revenge for what happened to Miller and Garrard. I could see the oil refinery with its guard towers from the trench, and there was no doubt in my mind the BOR security guards were working with AQI. The day went by quickly as we drove around the BOR interrogating the guards and any suspicious individuals, hoping someone could point us to the guys who blew up my brothers, but we had no luck.

We geared up for a night patrol. SSG Young and I led the "small kill team" on foot through a maze of gas pipes and fuel lines, looking for anyone who was stealing fuel. With our night vision on, and using hand and arm signals, we were invisible. Sometimes I was only a few feet away from an unsuspecting BOR security guard, watching him smoke a cigarette while chatting with his buddy, and they had no idea they were being watched by a team of killers, or that they had several carbines and machine guns with infrared lasers pointed at them.

We continued our patrol through the BOR when we reached a maze of gas pipes. As we made our way quietly through the maze, the point man raised his left arm, making a fist. We went prone and watched as four security guards filled several five-gallon jerry cans with gasoline. They had about twenty of those jugs waiting to be filled. Four men each grabbed two jugs and carried them to their truck and we got up and moved toward a wall where we took a knee, one behind another. I heard the voice of a guard grow louder as he made his way back to the jugs. When he appeared in front of me, I jumped out from behind the wall, covering his mouth with my left hand and grabbing his shirt with my right. I got him down on the ground, with his back to the wall, and placed the barrel of my M-4 on his chest.

"Shhh," I whispered to him with my left hand on his mouth and my right hand on the trigger. His eyes were wide, and he was terrified. I heard his friend calling for him, "Muhammad! Muhammad!" but he couldn't respond. When his buddy came looking for him, another team member grabbed him, put his hand on his mouth, and took him down. By this time, the other two Iraqis knew something was up, so our team came out from behind the wall and ordered them to drop to the ground. We zip-tied the four men and left two soldiers to watch them while we huddled in the distance.

"What are we gonna do with them?" I asked the team.

"Let's kill 'em," said another, and the rest of the team said "Yes!" in agreement.

"Where are we going to put their bodies?" I asked them.

"We can put their bodies in the oil field over there."

"It's too shallow, the stray dogs will go in there and eat them. Plus, if we shoot them, the officers back at the JSS will hear it."

"Okay, let's use knives. We can slit their throats." We all reached for our blades, ready to get our hands dirty.

"Wait. Again, where do we put their bodies?"

Damn. Why is this so complicated? I thought. I wanted revenge for Miller and Garrard but there were too many variables. Then I thought of something.

"What if we just beat the crap out of these guys." We all looked at each other and agreed that was the best course of action.

I took off my helmet, weapon, and body armor and placed them on the ground, and so did everyone else. We untied the Iraqis and stood them up.

"Alright, you ready?" one of my teammates said, and he got punched right in the jaw. The three other Iraqis tried briefly to put up a fight, but they got knocked out. I jumped on one of them, straddling his upper body in the full-mount, and started punching his face. After three clouts he was unconscious, but I kept hitting him. All of the rage I felt for what had happened to Miller and Garrard was crushing this guy's face. I could feel his cheekbones and his jaw breaking as my bare knuckles smashed into his face, again and again.

For a moment the thought, *I'm going to kill him,* went through my mind, but I kept hitting him anyway. I came down for another punch but when I connected to his face, I felt a sharp pain shoot up from my hand to my elbow. I looked at my hand and saw I had a golf ball size lump on my right hand, just below my pinky finger. I didn't know it yet, but I broke a bone. I got up, angry that my hand hurt, so I started kicking the guy's limp body, but even that hurt.

I was done beating people for the night, so I put my gear on and so did everyone else. I looked over at the Iraqis—their faces were bloodied and swollen from the beating. "I think we killed them," one soldier said as he walked toward the seemingly lifeless Iraqis. A few of the soldiers started shaking the security guards, but they weren't responding. I heard someone say, "Oh no! We need to hide their bodies." I stood over the guy whose face I destroyed, and he didn't appear to be breathing. I kneeled next to him and started violently shaking him.

"Hey! Wake up!"

He gasped for air and his chest started moving up and down, which was a good sign. He could barely see because his eyes were swollen so I helped him sit up. I poured water on his face and watched the blood drip down to his shirt. By then, his friends were awake but seriously beat up. I grabbed two gas cans and handed them to the guy I'd attacked, saying, "Here, you can have it. You paid for it, so enjoy it." He was afraid to touch the jugs. Maybe he thought we were going to beat him again. By this time, we all had our gear on, so we just put on our night vision and walked away, disappearing into the darkness.

When we returned to the JSS, Doc McClean wrapped my hand and gave me a Ziploc bag filled with ice. I took my gear off and sat down on a chair in front of a TV tuned to MTV, and a music video started playing. It was Nelly Furtado, and the song was titled, "Say It Right." The video began with a helicopter's propellers chopping the wind. That sound took me back to the dreaded medevac earlier that day.

I could see Miller and Garrard, cold and pale, asking for a woobie and begging to stay with us because they were warriors who did not want to be taken away. I watched the video as tears slowly filled my eyes and rolled down my cheeks. The hook of the song was, "You don't mean nothing at all to me."

For a moment, I felt alone. Yeah, I was a snake eater. I was a hunter of men, but no one back home knew or cared to know what we were doing. No one back home knew the constant danger we were in, or the friends I lost—warriors like SFC Knier, SGT Sigua, CPL Palmer, CPL Arvanitis, CSM Donovan Watts, and the others who gave their lives so their brothers could live. I thought about Miller and Garrard being wounded, and the operations we were carrying out every day and night. And again I told myself, *No one cares*. Not even God cared, I thought.

Tears rolled down my cheeks as the music video played and I nursed my hand with an ice pack.

But suddenly, I stopped feeling sorry for myself. I realized I wasn't alone. I was surrounded by the baddest dudes on the planet. I was a member of an elite team of killers who valued my life more than their own. And I valued their lives more than mine. This bond was more powerful than the bond I had with my biological family, even my mother. Whether I lived or died, I didn't care anymore. I was a snake eater, ready to sacrifice my life for my brothers, because they are all I had.

Eventually, God would show me I was wrong.

Chapter Thirty-Five

The Dark Side

SFC David A. Heringes
KIA 24 August 2007, Bayji, Iraq

I hated going to the motor pool, but it was something that we had to do, once a week, because our Humvees needed to be combat ready. I hated going to the motor pool for one reason, SFC Heringes. We all hated him. Everyone I talked to and everyone in our platoon hated Heringes. He was obnoxious to us all the time. I remember supervising the maintenance of our platoon Humvees and lining up in front of the motor pool, waiting for the mechanics to open shop. We were lined up after breakfast and Dusty, Taylor, and I were just talking and laughing as usual. We were joking around when a loud, angry scream interrupted our conversation.

"What the f--- are you doing?!" It was SFC Heringes and he was angry, as always. I didn't think he was yelling at me and my guys because we weren't doing anything wrong, so I looked around to see who he was yelling at. Other platoons from our battalion were also lined up outside the motor pool. I saw several other soldiers also looking around in bewilderment.

"What the f--- are you doing?!" he yelled again, but this time he was walking up to me.

"What's wrong, Sergeant?" I asked him.

"Your trucks need to be parked on the other side of this yellow line, you f-----' moron!" I looked down and saw that our trucks were slightly over the faded yellow line he was talking about.

"That's it!" he snapped, "Now you're going to be the last group we service today!" We arrived earlier to be first in line, and he was moving us to the back of the line because we were slightly over a faded yellow line. What an idiot.

What could have been a routine Humvee service lasting from 0900 to 1200, in time for us to get chow, turned into an all-day event, even though it was "first come, first serve," and we were first. And this wasn't the only time this happened—not by far. I'd had several encounters with Heringes and all of them were very much like the "yellow line" incident.

Everyone I talked to, even other mechanics, hated him with a passion. Every time someone was killed or wounded like Sigua, RV, CSM Watts, and the others, I always said, "Why is it that the good guys are getting killed and wounded? Why can't the turds die? Why is it always a squared-away, good guy? I hope Heringes dies!"

On August 24, 2007, my platoon and I returned from our three-day rotation at the BOR when we received word from our LT that another paratrooper was KIA. Our platoon was heartsick to hear this news. We stood with our heads down, looking to the ground, as the LT informed us of our unit's loss. Then he went on to tell us the paratrooper who was killed was SFC Heringes.

We all looked up in surprise.

Because Heringes was a mechanic, he often left the wire to recover Humvees severely damaged or destroyed. It turns out Heringes and another mechanic were called upon to recover a damaged vehicle using the M936 tow truck. Since the vehicle was on the shoulder of a road, the wrecker had to drive on the sand off the road for the wrecker to have the right angle to pull the Humvee onto the bed of the truck. SFC Heringes dismounted from the passenger side to ground guide the driver when he stepped on an anti-tank mine and was ripped in half.

Despite the tragic way he was killed, my feelings of sadness were quickly swept away by joy. At first I tried to hide it. I mean, how sick would I have to be to rejoice over a fellow paratrooper's death? But then I looked at the rest of my platoon and all of us were looking at each other as if seeking approval to rejoice. After Lt. Lukens informed us of Heringes's death, he walked away. My platoon stood in front of our CHUs (containerized housing units) waiting for the lieutenant to be out of hearing distance. In silence we stood in a horseshoe, and I thought about what we'd just learned. I wanted to mourn, and I even tried to make myself feel sad, but it wasn't working.

"Hell yeah!" our platoon broke out in celebration. "It's about time a loser dies and I'm glad it was him!" one paratrooper shouted in celebration. I wasn't the only one who was happy, but still I kept trying to hide my joy—even from myself. How could I be happy about this?

What had I become? Did I have a heart? Had three combat tours turned me into a heartless animal? These questions passed through my mind, but sorrow eluded me.

Our battalion held a memorial service on the FOB for SFC Heringes. No one in our platoon or soldiers in other companies wanted to go to the memorial service, but it was mandatory. As I walked with my platoon over to Globo Gym, I heard the murmuring voices of protest. "I have other things to do, like sleep, instead of going to this thing."

Somehow, it hurt me to hear these voices of protest, even though I felt the same way. I didn't want to go to this ceremony, and I didn't feel any sorrow over this death. The only remorse I felt was for not feeling remorse! I was wrestling within my heart trying to figure out what kind of person I was becoming. But the hard truth was I didn't care about human life the way I once did, and I didn't care about the Iraqi people. I came close to executing one Iraqi, and on every raid, I was looking for a reason to beat up or shoot anyone I encountered.

During the memorial service, a eulogy was given and two generals who flew in from the Green Zone were the first to walk up to the wooden box where SFC Heringes's rifle, boots, dog tags, and photo were placed. They stood at attention before the wooden box and, together, they brought their hands up to salute SFC Heringes. Once the two generals finished paying their respects, the rest of the battalion was welcomed to fall in line and pay respects.

"F--- that, I'm leaving," said one soldier from my platoon. Others said the same and, while some paratroopers lined up to pay their respects, I joined my platoon in walking out of Globo Gym without paying Heringes any final respect.

Still, as I walked away my mind was roiling with questions. *How messed up will I be by the time I get home? Am I going to die here? I don't think heaven is an option for me anymore. There's no way God will ever accept me, especially after I told Him I don't need Him anymore. Maybe I've crossed over to the dark side. Maybe I deserve to burn in hell.*

Chapter Thirty-Six

The Valley

ON OCTOBER 27, 2007, I returned to Fort Bragg, turned in my gear and headed back to the barracks. I was set to leave the Army on December 6, 2007, and I planned to begin college in January. That night, in the barracks, I woke up to the sound of an explosion. I was in the middle of a firefight and I could hear the bullets whizzing by my head as I dove to the barracks floor for cover. I was looking for my helmet, my body armor, and my weapon, but I couldn't find them.

I heard, "Bravo One-One, Bravo One-One, this is 1 Panther 71, over." I looked for the radio but I couldn't find it. I was on the tile floor of the barracks, with half of my body under my bed, when I looked up at a window and saw the barracks building next door and some trees. The firing and radio chatter stopped. I stood there in my barracks room, taking in deep breaths, waiting for my heart to stop racing.

This happened several nights.

After returning home, I stayed with my parents until I could find a place on my own. For the first three weeks, I lived out of my duffel bag I kept in the corner of my room just in case I got called back to war. Three weeks passed and there was no call. And the reality that I was no longer in the service started to sink in. I felt afraid. I was no longer with my brothers, whom I loved and trusted.

Who can I trust out here?

In college I excelled because I was disciplined. But every day, in the classroom or around campus, the same soundtrack played in my head. I could hear machine gun fire, mortars, and A-10's providing close air support. I carried a pistol with me. And when I returned home from school, if no one was home, I entered and cleared my house like I was entering an enemy-occupied building. Once it was clear, I turned on the TV, keeping the volume low so I could hear anyone attempting to sneak up on me. I kept the pistol on my lap.

I stayed in touch with Ascencio, my first team leader, and visited his home. He invited me to church and I met his minister, Pastor Joe. He was a heavyset white man, about seventy years old, with a white goatee. He looked like Santa Claus. The church welcomed me and I felt comfortable around Ascencio because we served together. Ascencio encouraged me to keep coming to church. But didn't know the battle I was facing inside, and I wasn't about to tell him.

Every weekend I went out with my brother and his friends, got drunk, then woke up Sunday morning, after about three hours of sleep, went to church, and sat in the back. I didn't sing, I didn't participate. I just sat there, hungover. But the more I went to church, the more I questioned whether I was living a good life.

More importantly, I questioned my relationship with God. I felt dirty. I carried the shame and guilt of knowing I hurt people in combat. I carried the shame of laughing when certain soldiers I didn't like were killed in action. "I'm a sick person. I'm ugly. I am unlovable." That was the script playing in my head. I was not worthy of God's love. But I kept going to church.

As time passed, I started feeling like I wasn't doing my part for the church. I showed up late, hungover. I sat there in silence, said "hi" to a few people, then went home to live like hell the rest of the week. I'd go out with friends and meet different girls. I found myself looking at them, and I thought, *These people are empty.* But no one felt more empty than I did.

Chapter Thirty-Seven

The War Within

ABOUT TWO YEARS after I left the Army, traumatic death experiences from combat came back to haunt me. I started having nightmares, and these were vivid dreams I thought were real. Sometimes they felt so real I checked my body for wounds after I woke up. But not all of them were about military experiences.

The most horrifying dream of all began when I found myself walking next to a barrel-chested man, who was wearing a red and black flannel shirt with faded blue overalls. He was about six-foot-five, and I couldn't see his face, but he was carrying a big black pig in his arms. The pig's nose was wet, and he snorted at me as I walked alongside the tall man toward a red barn.

The man was sturdy with big strong arms, featuring biceps the size of my head. The pig was a big one, and it must have weighed over 300 pounds. I couldn't see the man's face, and as I walked next to him my face was a little below his shoulders. He was huge.

Inside the barn, we walked up the stairs to a catwalk, I asked the man, "Where are we going?"

He answered, "We're going to feed the wolf."

We were looking down into the sealed-off portion of the barn, and suddenly I heard deep growling, fiercer than any dog could growl. It sent chills down my spine. The growling sounded evil, and I felt my heartbeat rise as fear fell over me. Below us, a stable door slowly opened as the wolf used his nose to push it as he slowly walked out. The wolf was black and had dark green eyes. He must have weighed over 200 pounds.

The wolf looked up and stared at the pig in the big man's arms and began to drool and lick his nose and front teeth, savoring the meal to come. The man threw the pig down from the catwalk and, without skipping a beat, the wolf sprinted to the pig and by the time the pig landed, the wolf was already on top of it. He sank his teeth into the pig's lower back as the pig squealed from the pain. The wolf devoured the pig.

The next thing I knew, the big man was telling me the wolf was just getting ready for the main course. Curious, I asked him, "What is the main course?"

With that he suddenly grabbed me with his huge, strong hands the size of a grizzly bear's paws. He picked me up and over the wooden rail of the wooden walkway we were standing on, and after a futile struggle on my part, he threw me to the wolf.

I fought the wild animal off, ripped out his heart, and killed him.

When I awoke, I was covered in sweat, sitting upright on my bed terrified. I could see the glowing green night sights on my pistol as I scanned my apartment for threats. It was just another nightmare, but I was more than sick of having nightmares. Some were replays of battles. Some were horror stories like that one. I was also beyond weary of sleeping less than three hours a night. The bitter truth was, I was tired of living.

I wept. "Lord, where are You?"

Chapter Thirty-Eight

The Angel Visits

AFTER FOUR YEARS of college, I graduated from the University of California Irvine with a bachelor's degree in criminology. I left the Army hoping to serve in law enforcement, but I was rejected by every law enforcement agency I applied to. I was rejected after admitting I carried a concealed firearm without a concealed carry permit, which is a felony in California. I applied for work at several retail stores, but no one showed interest in hiring me. I felt uncertain about my future. I was beginning to worry about how I would pay my rent or buy food, since I was living off the GI Bill and I was no longer a student.

One morning I went to the gym for a good workout to help me cope with stress. I felt much better after lifting weights and running on the indoor track. I left the gym and I drove back to my studio apartment. Normally, it was difficult to find parking in Long Beach because there were many apartments in my neighborhood. I looked for parking on the street in front of my apartment, but they were all taken. I made a right turn at the street corner and I saw there were several parking spaces on the opposite side of the street, in front of an elementary school. The parking spaces were slanted, so I would have to make a U-turn to park.

Before I made a U-turn, I noticed a man sitting on a bench in front of the school. He had brown hair, khaki pants, black dress shoes, a tucked-in flannel shirt, and a brown polyester jacket. We locked eyes and he quickly gathered what looked like several newspapers he had on the bench, next to his lap. I wondered if I knew who he was because the way he locked eyes with me and gathered his things was as if he was waiting for me. It seemed like he knew I was going to park in front of the school. He even smiled when our eyes met, like he was happy to see me.

I parked my truck and noticed he was calmly walking toward me, waiting to meet me when I stepped out. *Great, another homeless guy who thinks that I have money to give away.* I grabbed my gym towel, keys, and wallet, and I planned on walking away without talking to this stranger. He stood on the sidewalk on the passenger side of my truck, so when I stepped out from the driver side, I began to walk hurriedly away, hoping to avoid any encounter with him

"Excuse me, brother." His gentle voice was odd, and I wondered why he called me brother.

I turned around and said, "What's up?"

He was a short man, about 5'5" with a receding hairline. His mustache was well trimmed so I could see his top lip and all his teeth as he smiled. "Brother, I've been up since 5 a.m. looking for a job. I live at the shelter nearby and I've been giving out my résumé to every fast-food place and anyone who is hiring." The man unrolled the newspapers he was carrying, and he showed me the many classified ads he highlighted and several copies of his résumé.

"Sorry, but I don't have any money," I told him, and then I proceeded to walk away.

"Brother," he said gently, "I don't want any money from you; but I haven't had anything to eat since five this morning and it's now 2:30 in the afternoon. I was wondering, could you please give me something to eat?" He held the folded newspapers with both of his hands, and he slightly bowed his head in humility.

"You want something to eat?" I asked him bluntly.

"Brother, I would really appreciate it if you gave me something to eat, even if it's just a piece of bread."

"Okay," I said, "come with me."

We entered my studio apartment and walked into the kitchen. I started cooking some food. I could hear the man singing a Christian hymn, "Jesus, Your Name Is Power." I placed a salmon in the oven and sat across from him at my small kitchen table.

"Are you a Christian?" I asked him.

"Yes, brother. I love Jesus Christ."

I asked him what his name was, but I don't remember it. I told him I was also a believer and he rejoiced. "Praise the Lord." His eyes began to water, and I could see he was filled with joy as he kept quietly singing the song.

"Brother," he abruptly stopped singing. "I hate to ask you for more because you've done so much for me, but . . ." he took off his dress shoes and continued, "I don't have any socks. I have been walking all day and I have blisters on my feet. Can you please give me a pair of socks?" I saw the blisters on both of his feet. This man had clearly been walking for a long time.

"No problem," I told him, and I got up and walked over to my dresser. I gave him a thick pair of boot socks.

"Praise the Lord, brother." I watched as tears rolled down his cheeks in joy. He put the socks on his feet and then a look of relief came over his face. "Brother, I hate to ask you for more. I'm sorry, brother, but there's something that I need more than the food you have in the oven." I was still skeptical about this man's true intentions, and I suspected that at some point he was going to ask me for money. "So what is it that you need?" I asked in a low voice.

"Sorry to ask you for so much, but what I need is the Word of God. Do you have a Bible you can give me?" I wish he asked me for money. I didn't realize how precious the Bible was to me until I was asked to give mine to someone else. I had two Bibles, and I didn't want to give them up. I paused for a moment as I thought about how to respond.

"Okay, I have two Bibles," I told him, and I'll give you one of them."

The look of joy over this poor man's face showed his genuine love for the Lord. I walked into my living room, to my computer desk where I had my Bibles resting on top. I grabbed one of them, walked back over to the kitchen and gave it to him. He opened the Bible to Acts 5:40–42 and he read it aloud.

"They took his advice; and after calling the apostles in, they flogged them and ordered them not to speak in the name of Jesus, and then released them. So they went on their way from the presence of the Council, rejoicing that they had been considered worthy to suffer shame for His name. And every day, in the temple and from house to house, they kept right on teaching and preaching Jesus as the Christ" (NASB).

"So no matter what you face in the future, God is faithful, and He will get you through."

I didn't think much about what he said because the food was ready. I grabbed some plates, pulled the salmon out of the oven, and served us both. I prayed over our meal and we ate. As we ate, the man asked me, "Where do you work?"

I told him I just finished school and wanted to be a police officer, but no department would hire me. I shared with him how I, like him, was also looking for a job.

"Brother, God has a job for you. The job may not be what you wanted but God will bless you."

We finished eating and we talked for a little while and then he told me he had to leave. He was going to a job interview and he asked me to pray for him. I prayed for him and then walked him out to the alley behind my apartment. As we stood in the alley the man looked down at the Bible I gave him, and he smiled. "Thank you for everything, brother."

"You're welcome. If you're ever around, you're welcome to come by."

"Thanks, brother."

Before he left, he said, "Remember, God has a plan for you. God has a job for you. You may suffer and life can be hard, but God is with you."

I thanked him, and we hugged. I watched him walk down the street, then he made a right turn on the corner. I decided to follow him to see where he was going, so I sprinted to the street corner. When I got there, I looked for him, but he was gone. I walked for half a block, trying to see where he might have gone, but there was no place for him to disappear. He was gone and I never saw or heard from him again. It was like he vanished.

The following day, my phone rang.

"Hello," I answered.

"Hi, may I speak with Fernando Arroyo?"

"This is Fernando," I replied.

"Fernando, I'd like for you to come in for an interview."

It was too good to be true.

"Okay," I said. "I'll be there tomorrow."

"Sounds good. Be here at 10 a.m. I'm looking forward to meeting you. See you tomorrow."

"See you tomorrow. Thank you."

Chapter Thirty-Nine

Wholesale

I WAS HIRED as a shopping cart collector and I hated it. I spent my time in a hot parking lot under a scorching sun, where temperatures sometimes reached 100 degrees. All day I worked hard to make sure there were shopping carts available for the customers while also stopping to help them load heavy merchandise in their cars. One day I helped a woman and I noticed a UC Irvine bumper sticker.

"Did you go to UCI?"

"No, my son graduated from there."

"Me too."

"What do you mean?" She looked confused.

"I graduated from UCI too."

"Then, why are you working here?" Then she walked away with a disgusted look on her face. She probably thought I was lying.

I was angry and felt humiliated. Why wouldn't anyone hire me? I applied for several government jobs (unrelated to law enforcement) and I was rejected by all of them. Once again I began to question God. I was so unhappy working as a shopping cart collector, but it was the only job I could find. And of the few other jobs I was offered, collecting shopping carts paid the most, even though it wasn't much.

I returned home after another long and miserable day and grabbed my mail. It contained two letters from two police departments. I was excited to open them and find out which one wanted to hire me. I ripped open one of them and the first words I read were, "We are sorry . . ." I tore open the second letter, hopeful this was going to be my ticket out of the shopping cart business. The letter began with, "We regret to inform you . . ."

Rejected again.

The next day I went to work and it was one of the hottest days ever. People must've thought I was crazy because I was talking to God (quietly) the whole time, and I wasn't exactly praising Him. "Is this your 'master plan,' God? Really? Is this the best You can do?"

Over the months I attended church; I helped frequently with the Sunday services. After a while, I was even asked to speak to the congregation. I never said a word about myself, my wartime experiences, or my struggles. But people seemed to like it when I talked about Bible passages and simple truths I learned from them.

Later that day I received a phone call during my break and heard that Pastor Joe had pneumonia and was at the hospital. The church was small, about fifty people, and Ascencio was working that Sunday, so everyone at church was hoping I would speak at the Sunday service. I reluctantly agreed. But at the same time I continued to complain to God about the mess He was permitting in my life.

I was returning shopping carts next to the front door when I saw the warehouse manager walking toward me. *I'm getting fired. Great! Now I can find another job*, I said, sarcastically to myself.

"Hey, you got a minute?" Mike asked.

"Sure."

"So do you like collecting carts?"

"Huh?"

"Yeah, do you like collecting carts? Honestly. I did it when I first started working for the company. I hated it."

"Yeah, I hate it."

"Well, all the managers speak highly of you. They say you're the best cart guy ever. But I thought, yeah but he doesn't belong where he is. So I think you should be doing something else."

"Oh yeah? Like what?"

"Like driving a truck. We need delivery drivers and I think you should do that instead. We'll train you and pay for you to get a commercial driver's license. It pays more than this."

"Okay. I'll do it."

Chapter Forty

The End of Myself

ONE DAY I was driving to make a delivery when I was overcome with sadness. I started weeping uncontrollably, and I had to pull over on a street in West Los Angeles. It wasn't the first time this happened. This was becoming a weekly occurrence, sometimes twice a week. Any song, sight, or smell that reminded me of Iraq or Afghanistan, and brought back memories of my fallen brothers, or the many tragedies I experienced in combat, would trigger a panic attack type response. I would cry uncontrollably and have to pull over on the side of the road, trying not to get into an accident while driving with tear-blurred eyes. For the last year I was falling apart. I hated the fact I was a delivery driver. I was rejected by every police department I applied to. The plans that I had of being married, having children, serving in law enforcement, and buying a home, did not pan out.

At the same time, almost every night I was gripped by vivid nightmares, and averaging three hours of sleep per night. To help myself sleep, I started drinking alcohol every night until I passed out. More and more I felt like I was being consumed by a dark force taking me by night, but now also creeping up on me in the light of day. I often had uncontrollable crying spells in the daytime, then terrible nightmares whenever I finally got to sleep.

I was broken.

When I left the Army, I attended church every Sunday, but I did not feel a sense of community. Going to church was more of a Sunday routine. I would greet all the same people, participate in church service, and say goodbye, only to repeat the same routine the next week. I didn't trust the church members enough to let them know what pain I was harboring within me. I left the band of brothers I had in the Army. The brothers who would lay down their lives for me. The brothers who faced the enemy, time and time again, alongside me. I felt alone.

One day I went home after work and started drinking. I drank beer after beer all night long until I drifted off to sleep, only to have another nightmare wake me up, terrified.

I opened another beer and started questioning God all over again. "Why did You keep me alive?" I asked Him. "I trusted You, Lord, and You failed me. You should have let me die in Iraq."

I walked back to my bed and grabbed the pistol from under the pillow. I pulled the slide back to see if there was a round in the chamber, and there was. With the pistol in one hand and a beer in another, I sat on the sofa. Tears began to roll down my cheeks as I reflected on the possibility of killing myself

The best days of life are behind me, I thought. *I've lived a good life. I served in combat, I jumped out of airplanes, I finished Ranger School, so I've done a lot. I have a bachelor's degree and I even preach at church. I help people. Maybe it's time for me to go. My life isn't getting any better. And if I die now, I'll finish strong.*

I chugged on the beer, and the bottle fell out of my hand when I finished it.

As I wrote at the beginning of this book, on that terrible night the pistol blurred through my tears as I held it in front of me and turned it toward my face. I was holding it with both hands. The barrel was as wide as my right eye. The tears kept flowing from my eyes, across my cheeks and down my chin. I gently inserted the pistol into my mouth with both hands still on the pistol grip.

Click—the sound of the safety lever being deactivated by my right thumb was loud in the quiet apartment. I could smell and taste the pistol lubricant as I deeply inhaled and exhaled. I placed my right thumb on the trigger and let it sit there.

God, if You're there, save me! I said in my mind hoping God would hear my silent plea, but there was no response. I slowly began to apply pressure to the trigger. I wanted the explosion to be a surprise.

Bang!

I was gripped with fear and dropped the pistol. My eyes flew open and I looked around me. There was no blood. I touched the back of my head to see what damage the gunshot did. There was no wound. I was confused, so I started looking around my living room, wondering what that terrifying sound might been.

Then I saw it—my Bible was on the floor. It somehow flew off my office desk and hit the floor so hard it sounded like a gunshot.

I got down on my knees, crying to God. "Lord, help me. I can't do this anymore. I give up. My life is Yours. Please, Lord, save me."

Chapter Forty-One

The Road to Redemption

THE NEXT DAY I received a phone call from my old high school friend, Luis España. He found a career with the Department of Veterans Affairs (VA) in West Los Angeles, and it was his job to help veterans receive the help they needed. He wanted me to get connected with the VA. At first, I rejected his offer. But after a few days of his persistent calling and text messaging thinking I needed help—even offering to pick me up, buy me breakfast, and take me to the VA—I finally said "yes."

I filled out all the necessary paperwork and was quickly scheduled to meet with a clinical social worker at an East Los Angeles VA clinic. I arrived early and was given a packet to fill out, containing a mental health evaluation form. I was asked questions about my combat experience, drinking habits, and traumatic events. I lied answering almost every question, turned in the packet to the receptionist, and waited for my turn.

A bald man, about forty-five years old with a dark goatee walked up to greet me. "Hi, my name is Bob Wymms and I'm a clinical social worker. Let's step into my office."

I shook his hand and followed him. I sat down on a chair next to his desk and we went over my packet.

"Well, according to your answers, you don't need our help. It looks like you're doing just fine.

"Awesome. Am I free to go?"

"Well—let's talk a little."

I was already halfway out of my chair when he said we should talk. So I sat back down and waited for him to begin.

"I'm having trouble believing you were honest in answering these questions. Your answers indicate you're fine, but your military history tells me something else. Your DD 214 shows me you were in the Airborne Infantry, you served on three deployments, graduated Ranger School and you were awarded the Combat Infantryman's Badge. Your military history does not match your answers."

I didn't say anything. I kept a poker face and waited for him to speak first.

"Fernando, what I'm saying is, I think you're full of s--t," he said with a smile. "Look, I am here to help you. Whatever you share here, stays here. I am for you; I am not against you. Even if you confess that you committed murder, it will stay between us."

Silence filled the room. *Damn, can I trust this guy?* I thought.

"If I ask you some questions, will you answer them truthfully?"

I hesitated to respond to his question because I didn't know if I could trust him. *Should I leave, or should I be honest?* I debated with myself for a few seconds and then finally answered.

"Okay."

"Did you lose any friends in combat?"

"Yes."

"Did you ever have to shoot someone when you were in combat?"

"Yes."

"Do you have nightmares?"

"Yes."

"About how many hours of sleep are you getting each night?"

"Three."

"Have you thought about suicide?"

"Yes."

"Have you ever attempted suicide?"

"Yes."

"Do you drink alcohol?"

"Yes."

"Did you drink any alcohol on Friday?"

"Yes."

"About how many drinks did you have Friday?"

"Thirty."

"Who were you with?"

"Alone."

"How about Saturday?"

"Thirty."

"Who were you with on Saturday?"

"Alone."

Bob leaned forward on his chair and looked me in the eyes, "Fernando, you need help."

So, I finally admitted I had a problem. I couldn't run anymore. I'd hid my pain from my family, I'd hid my pain from my church, but I couldn't hide my pain from God. God brought me to a point of surrender. It was time to face my past. It was time for me to confess my sins. I agreed to meet with Bob twice a week for the first several months and then once a week after that, over the span of one year.

That weekend I received a call from Bob. I knew I was messed up because Bob called me on his day off to ask me a simple question.

"Hey, Bob."

"Fernando, are you having any thoughts of suicide?"

"No. Not today."

"Are you sober?"

"Yes, I'm sober."

"Okay, good. I just called to make sure you were okay. I hope you have a great weekend."

I walked into Bob's office the following Monday and sat on the chair next to his desk. I made it a point to be honest. I was done hiding. I was done hiding my nightmares, I was done hiding my guilt and my shame, and I was done feeling like I was a disgusting human being for the things I did in combat. I sat with Bob twice a week and I answered every question truthfully. I shared some of the most difficult things I was dealing with.

I talked to Bob about SFC Heringes. I felt guilt and shame for being happy he died and continued to feel like a disgusting human being for never paying my respects to him. It felt good to have someone who listened to me as I shared my emotional burdens I had been carrying for several years. And as time passed, I came to the realization I really wasn't a disgusting person. The fact I felt guilt and shame meant I knew what I did was wrong. Meaning I had a conscience. Instead of living with conviction, I learned conviction was meant to lead me to repentance.

"Fernando, do you believe in God?" Bob asked.

"Yes."

"Okay. What religion do you identify with? If you don't mind me asking."

"I'm a Christian."

"Okay. Well, why did Christ die on the cross?"

"For the forgiveness of our sins."

"Well, do you believe God will forgive you if you ask Him to?"

My vision blurred as I fought hard to hold back the tears flooding my eyes. I looked down, feeling ashamed I was tearing up in front of another man.

"Fernando, there is no shame in crying. Even Jesus wept."

With that, I couldn't hold back my tears and I watched as they splashed on the tile floor. I remembered watching my sweat turn into puddles on the shiny barracks hallway floor for so many years, but now it was my tears. Bob wasn't a Christian, but he invited me to pray to Christ and he would respectfully listen.

I prayed to Jesus and brought my burdens to the foot of the cross. I laid my burdens at His feet and I understood, once again, what it meant to be redeemed. I was not an evil man. I was just a soldier, a paratrooper, trying to survive in a war zone. We live in a fallen world and it is unfortunate that men and women must stand up to fight against evil, but the lines get blurry when you get blood on your hands.

I started to question whether I was just as evil as the men I was fighting. I now realized I was not. I confronted evil people and defeated them. To cope with the stress of seeing so much death and violence, I created a mindset where I tried to hide my fears and my emotions, because I feared facing them. Well, now I was facing them. Like the warrior God called me to be, I faced my fears and my emotions with a broken and contrite heart.

And I was redeemed.

I reflected on my past and found where I went wrong. I moved from trusting in God and His strength when I was a child and through basic and airborne training, to following my own desires and allowing my pride to take His place. I relied on my accomplishments and I relied on my military training, believing my identity was found in my uniform, but it wasn't. I had a void in my heart I, like so many people, tried to fill with the things of this world, only to realize the void in my heart could only be filled by God. My identity was found in Him and not in anything else.

I made it a point to visit the graves of my fallen brothers, going on road trips across the country. I shed tears at their tombstones, and was not ashamed of it. I still cry sometimes when I hear a song or watch a movie that reminds me of them. That is how I honor them. I honor them by remembering them and I honor them by living the best life I can possibly live. I know my fallen comrades would not want me to live in misery for the rest of my life.

I felt God's call on my life to help those who served. Through the process of getting help for my past trauma, I enrolled in seminary at BIOLA University. While earning my Master of Divinity (MDiv) in pastoral care and counseling, I worked with other veterans and staff members to establish the BIOLA Veterans Association and create a family of God-fearing veterans on campus. In October of 2019, Biola University opened its doors to the new Biola Veterans Center. Now, veterans transitioning out of the military and onto Biola's campus, will have the community many veterans lack.

I completed my MDiv in May of 2019, and today I work at the Orange County Rescue Mission (OCRM) as the veteran services case manager. These days I help homeless and other veterans establish a relationship with God. We work together to break the chains of homelessness, alcohol and drug addiction, and post-traumatic stress.

I attend Mariners Church in Orange County, California, and I participate in men's groups and Bible studies. We were not made to live life alone. We were made for community. First, community with God and second, community with friends and family.

I couldn't see it when I was in combat, losing friends and wondering what my future had in store. I couldn't see it when I was in negative five-degree temperatures wondering if I had what it takes to earn the Ranger Tab. I couldn't see it when I lost the woman I thought I loved, and was heartbroken. I couldn't see how God was with me the whole time.

He kept me through it all and every moment of pain, emotional, psychological, and spiritual, was meant to mold me and prepare me so I could serve in His kingdom ministering to the veteran community. And now I'm seeking to live a life that honors my fallen brothers and sisters, and a life that honors God.

I almost ended my life. Now, I live to save lives. To every veteran who reads this: you are loved by God! Your life is worth living! Even if I've never met you, I am able to understand your struggle. I care about you and I want to encourage you to live a life that honors our fallen veterans, and most of all to live a life that honors God. Amen.